OPPOSING
VIEWPOINTS®
SERIES

Gangs

Other Books of Related Interest:

Opposing Viewpoints Series

America's Youth

Teens at Risk

Violence

At Issue Series

Guns and Crime

Teen Smoking

Teen Suicide

Contemporary Issues Companion

Gun Violence

Current Controversies Series

Anger Management

Family Violence

Guns and Violence

"Congress shall make no law . . . abridging the freedom of speech, or of the press."

First Amendment to the U.S. Constitution

The basic foundation of our democracy is the First Amendment guarantee of freedom of expression. The Opposing Viewpoints Series is dedicated to the concept of this basic freedom and the idea that it is more important to practice it than to enshrine it.

Gangs

Adela Soliz, Book Editor

GREENHAVEN PRESS
A part of Gale, Cengage Learning

Detroit • New York • San Francisco • New Haven, Conn • Waterville, Maine • London

Christine Nasso, *Publisher*
Elizabeth Des Chenes, *Managing Editor*

© 2009 Greenhaven Press, a part of Gale, Cengage Learning.

Gale and Greenhaven Press are registered trademarks used herein under license.

For more information, contact:
Greenhaven Press
27500 Drake Rd.
Farmington Hills, MI 48331-3535
Or you can visit our Internet site at gale.cengage.com

For product information and technology assistance, contact us at

Gale Customer Support, 1-800-877-4253
For permission to use material from this text or product, submit all requests online at www.cengage.com/permissions

Further permissions questions can be emailed to permissionrequest@cengage.com

Articles in Greenhaven Press anthologies are often edited for length to meet page requirements. In addition, original titles of these works are changed to clearly present the main thesis and to explicitly indicate the author's opinion. Every effort is made to ensure that Greenhaven Press accurately reflects the original intent of the authors. Every effort has been made to trace the owners of copyrighted material.

Cover photograph reproduced by permission of Image copyright STILLFX, 2009. Used under license from Shutterstock.com.

LIBRARY OF CONGRESS CATALOGING-IN-PUBLICATION DATA

Gangs / Adela Soliz, book editor.
    p. cm. -- (Opposing viewpoints)
    Includes bibliographical references and index.
    ISBN-13: 978-0-7377-4366-1 (hbk.)
    ISBN-13: 978-0-7377-4365-4 (pbk.)
    1. Gangs--United States--Juvenile literature. 2. Gangs--Juvenile literature.
 I. Soliz, Adela.
    HV6439.U5G3586 2009
    364.1'0660973--dc22

                                                  2009010705

Printed in the United States of America
1 2 3 4 5 6 7 13 12 11 10 09

Contents

Why Consider Opposing Viewpoints?   11

Introduction   14

Chapter 1: How Widespread Is the Problem of Gangs?

Chapter Preface   19

1. Girl Membership in Gangs Is on the Rise   21
   Eloisa Ruano Gonzalez

2. The Problem of Girl Gangs Has Been Exaggerated   28
   Joan Smith

3. Gangs Are a Problem of the Underprivileged   34
   Ely Flores

4. Privileged Children Also Get Involved in Gangs   41
   Gillian Flaccus

5. Immigration Contributes to the Gang Problem   45
   Brian R. Ballou and Maria Sacchetti

6. Immigrants Are Not Responsible for Increases in Criminal Activity   51
   The Economist

Periodical Bibliography   55

Chapter 2: Why Do People Join Gangs?

Chapter Preface   57

1. Adolescents Join Gangs for a Sense of Social Belonging   59
   Phelan Wyrick

2. Victims of Violent Crimes Join Gangs   66
   Terrance J. Taylor

3. The Rap Industry Exacerbates the Gang Problem 73
   Donald Lyddane

4. The Relationship Between Rap and Gangs 80
   Has Been Misunderstood
   John M. Hagedorn

5. Gangs Are Proliferating in Prisons 89
   Michael Montgomery

6. Prison Managers Are Effectively Fighting 99
   the Proliferation of Gangs in Prisons
   Ron Holvey

Periodical Bibliography 107

Chapter 3: What Should Be Done to Prevent Gangs?

Chapter Preface 109

1. State Lawmakers Are Helping to Prevent Gangs 111
   Sarah Hammond

2. Policy Makers and Police Do Not Help 117
   Prevent Gangs
   Judith Greene and Kevin Pranis

3. Police Do Not Effectively Combat Gangs 128
   Trymaine Lee

4. Gang Prevention Programs That 136
   Offer Alternatives to Youth Will Decrease
   Gang Activity
   Irving A. Spergel

5. Many Gang Prevention Programs Have 150
   Not Been Proven Effective
   Delbert S. Elliot

Periodical Bibliography 159

Chapter 4: What Is the Impact of Gangs?

Chapter Preface   **161**

1. Gangs Have a Large Economic Impact   **163**
   Fight Crime: Invest in Kids

2. Gangs Often Traffic in Drugs   **170**
   Nicholas V. Lampson

3. Not All Gang Members Are Involved in Drugs   **175**
   Trevor Bennett and Katy Holloway

4. Gangs Disrupt Schools   **183**
   Susannah Rosenblatt

5. Gangs Do Not Increase Violence in Schools   **188**
   Sarah Schmidt

Periodical Bibliography   **192**

For Further Discussion   **193**

Organizations to Contact   **196**

Bibliography of Books   **202**

Index   **206**

Why Consider
Opposing Viewpoints?

> *"The only way in which a human being
> can make some approach to knowing the
> whole of a subject is by hearing what
> can be said about it by persons of every
> variety of opinion and studying all
> modes in which it can be looked at by
> every character of mind. No wise man
> ever acquired his wisdom in any mode
> but this."*
>
> *John Stuart Mill*

In our media-intensive culture it is not difficult to find differing opinions. Thousands of newspapers and magazines and dozens of radio and television talk shows resound with differing points of view. The difficulty lies in deciding which opinion to agree with and which "experts" seem the most credible. The more inundated we become with differing opinions and claims, the more essential it is to hone critical reading and thinking skills to evaluate these ideas. Opposing Viewpoints books address this problem directly by presenting stimulating debates that can be used to enhance and teach these skills. The varied opinions contained in each book examine many different aspects of a single issue. While examining these conveniently edited opposing views, readers can develop critical thinking skills such as the ability to compare and contrast authors' credibility, facts, argumentation styles, use of persuasive techniques, and other stylistic tools. In short, the Opposing Viewpoints Series is an ideal way to attain the higher-level thinking and reading skills so essential in a culture of diverse and contradictory opinions.

In addition to providing a tool for critical thinking, Opposing Viewpoints books challenge readers to question their own strongly held opinions and assumptions. Most people form their opinions on the basis of upbringing, peer pressure, and personal, cultural, or professional bias. By reading carefully balanced opposing views, readers must directly confront new ideas as well as the opinions of those with whom they disagree. This is not to simplistically argue that everyone who reads opposing views will—or should—change his or her opinion. Instead, the series enhances readers' understanding of their own views by encouraging confrontation with opposing ideas. Careful examination of others' views can lead to the readers' understanding of the logical inconsistencies in their own opinions, perspective on why they hold an opinion, and the consideration of the possibility that their opinion requires further evaluation.

Evaluating Other Opinions

To ensure that this type of examination occurs, Opposing Viewpoints books present all types of opinions. Prominent spokespeople on different sides of each issue as well as well-known professionals from many disciplines challenge the reader. An additional goal of the series is to provide a forum for other, less known, or even unpopular viewpoints. The opinion of an ordinary person who has had to make the decision to cut off life support from a terminally ill relative, for example, may be just as valuable and provide just as much insight as a medical ethicist's professional opinion. The editors have two additional purposes in including these less known views. One, the editors encourage readers to respect others' opinions—even when not enhanced by professional credibility. It is only by reading or listening to and objectively evaluating others' ideas that one can determine whether they are worthy of consideration. Two, the inclusion of such viewpoints encourages the important critical thinking skill of objectively evaluating an author's credentials and bias. This evaluation will illuminate an author's reasons for taking a particular stance on an issue and will aid in readers' evaluation of the author's ideas.

It is our hope that these books will give readers a deeper understanding of the issues debated and an appreciation of the complexity of even seemingly simple issues when good and honest people disagree. This awareness is particularly important in a democratic society such as ours in which people enter into public debate to determine the common good. Those with whom one disagrees should not be regarded as enemies but rather as people whose views deserve careful examination and may shed light on one's own.

Thomas Jefferson once said that "difference of opinion leads to inquiry, and inquiry to truth." Jefferson, a broadly educated man, argued that "if a nation expects to be ignorant and free . . . it expects what never was and never will be." As individuals and as a nation, it is imperative that we consider the opinions of others and examine them with skill and discernment. The Opposing Viewpoints Series is intended to help readers achieve this goal.

David L. Bender and Bruno Leone,
Founders

Introduction

"The fact that Mexico—which has historically been averse to any assistance from the U.S. that could be construed as a breach of its sovereignty—is seeking the increased aid shows how serious a threat President Felipe Calderón sees drug gangs posing to his country."

Howard LaFranchi,
Christian Science Monitor

Gangs and gang violence affect all types of people. Gangs recruit both boys and girls; gangs plague suburban as well as urban communities; and gangs are not just a problem in the United States. In fact gangs, like the economic crisis of 2008, global warming, and terrorism, are an international problem. Nothing makes the international nature of the gang problem clearer than the war Mexico is currently waging against the heavily armed drug gangs that have been brutally murdering each other and terrorizing civilians. Mexico's gang war could be said to have officially started in December of 2006 when newly inaugurated Mexican president Felipe Calderón sent federal troops to six of Mexico's states to fight the drug gangs. Though most of the violence during the first two years of this war from 2006 to 2008 has been confined to Mexican soil, at least three factors make this as much the United States' problem as it is Mexico's. First, the United States is the primary market for the drugs being transported and sold by these Mexican gangs and so in a sense these drug gangs exist because of the market created by the United States. Second, drug gangs have started to terrorize American immigration officers working along the border and may be hiring members of street gangs in the interior of the United States to sell their drugs. Finally, in December of 2008 the United States released the first part of an aid package to Mexico intended to help Mexican federal troops become as well trained and armed as the gangs they are fighting.

Drugs are at the root of the Mexican gang problem. Before the military intervened in 2006, much of the violence associated with these gangs was a result of rival gangs fighting over key drug territory. According to Phoebe Powell in a December 15, 2008, article for Canada's *National Post*, "90% of all drugs that enter the United States are from Mexican cartels. Cocaine is the main import. Mexico is also the source of almost all the methamphetamine consumed in the United States." Furthermore, the very valuable nature of the drug trade may be what's fueling the brutality of these gangs. An anonymous newspaper editor in the Mexican state of Chihuahua, speaking to the *National Post*, observed, "This war should stop when consumer nations stop buying narcotics. While the internal consumptions of drugs in Mexico is becoming larger, most of the drugs ... are sent to the United States. It's a huge market that encourages criminals to take larger risks." Drug use in the United States is an underlying reason for the gang problem in both the United States and Mexico. The problems of drug use and gangs are intertwined and gangs can not be eradicated until the problem of drug use is solved.

The drug business of Mexico's gangs is transnational and now the violence is spreading across the border. Fear of Mexico's drug war is increasing as citizens witness the violence moving onto U.S. soil. Violence from Mexico's drug gangs has begun to threaten border patrol agents as well as people who live along the Mexican border. In a January 2009 article the *Washington Times* reported: "near-daily shootouts and ambushes along the southwestern border pose a serious threat, according to separate government reports, which predict a rise in 'deadly force' against law enforcement officers, first responders and U.S. border residents." Mexico's drug war may not only affect immigrants and residents who cross the border, the fear that it causes may lead to far-reaching changes in immigration and national security policy. Politicians who previously took liberal views of immigration policy may start to support more conservative border protection methods in order to protect their constituents. U.S. Representative Louie Gohmert of Texas speaking before the House Subcommittee on Crime, Terrorism, and Homeland Security in June 2008 argued, "violent international gangs, such as MS-13, or border gangs, such as Los Zetas, pose a dangerous threat that requires a sophisticated coordinated law enforcement response . . . one tactic must be mandatory, and that is for greater border security at a time when the estimates we have heard indicate that there may be 70 to 75 percent of gang members illegally here in this country."

Finally, Mexico and the United States have become partners in pursuit of this gang problem because of the aid package the United States is sending to Mexico. The aid package is intended to help Mexico's military purchase weaponry and fund training that will level the playing field between them and the more sophisticated muscle of the gangs. American aid will also be used to help Mexico reform its judiciary system. However, some argue that the aid should really be used to root out the corruption in Mexico's political system because if this is not done then no other efforts to stop Mexico's gangs will succeed. *The Economist* argues, "Few doubt the goodwill of Mr. Calderón or his top law-enforcement lieutenants, who are widely respected by their American counterparts. But down the chain of command, corruption remains the rule rather than the exception, and many doubt that the new measures will be able to change that."

The problem of gangs is widespread and affects many different aspects of society. Gangs contribute to societal diseases such as violence and drug addiction, they affect immigration policy, and they are part of the international political agenda.

In *Opposing Viewpoints: Gangs,* the contributors explore gangs in the following chapters: How Widespread Is the Problem of Gangs? Why Do People Join Gangs? What Should Be Done to Prevent Gangs? and What Is the Impact of Gangs? The authors demonstrate in their answers to these questions that gangs are a multifaceted and pertinent issue in today's society.

How Widespread Is
the Problem of Gangs?

Chapter Preface

The word "gangs" may bring up mental images of graffiti-covered subway tunnels in New York City or crews of young men walking the poorer streets of Los Angeles. Gangs used to be a problem of large urban communities. However, law enforcement officials and community members are witnessing gangs moving from large cities such as Chicago, Los Angeles, and New York to the surrounding suburbs.

According to *Organized Crime Digest*, Chicago Police Department's Area Gun Teams have established that there is a growing gang presence in the suburbs. They make this claim based on reports given by community members and testimonies of offenders picked up on gun possession or drug-related charges. Ethan Wilensky-Lanford reporting for the *New York Times* has evidence from law enforcement officers of the presence of gangs in suburban communities. After describing a drive-by shooting in the suburban town of Ewing, New Jersey, Wilensky-Lanford goes on to state, "the police said at least half of the 14 homicides committed in the city this year were tied to gangs. The city of 84,000 has 2,000 documented gang members, according to police officials." Thus, even in the small town of Ewing the crime rate is doubled because of gang activity. A security officer who works at a high school in the affluent Los Angeles community of Pasadena gave further evidence that gangs have a strong presence in the suburbs. He told the *Los Angeles Sentinel*, "the real violence [youths in Pasadena] experience is because of the increasing number of gang members from urban communities expanding their territory to the suburbs."

Dan Korem, author of *Suburban Gangs*, argues that it is not that gangs are expanding from large urban centers into the suburbs, but rather that affluent youths are forming their own gangs. Korem, who lives in a Dallas suburb, observes,

"Just a couple of months ago after one of my son's football games, two suburban kids associated with gangs drew guns, pointing them at each other's heads—not in a dark, blighted neighborhood, but in front of a local pizza parlor."

It is also argued that gangs are a growing presence in the suburbs because as more people move from the cities to the suburbs, problems such as racial alienation, lack of jobs, and poor education have started to affect the suburbs almost as much as the inner city. "I feel that it's a combination of the education system, lack of jobs and a lack of skills to enable men and women to be competitive [in their new surroundings]," says Pasadena councilwoman Jacque Robinson in the *Los Angeles Sentinel*. In the following chapters the authors debate the extent of the gang problem, who they are, and which communities are affected by them.

> *"Mike Fairbanks, a Yakima County juvenile probation officer who works out of Sunnyside and oversees many gang members who've gone through the detention center, notices more girls have been recruited lately."*

Girl Membership in Gangs Is on the Rise

Eloisa Ruano Gonzalez

In the following viewpoint, Eloisa Ruano Gonzalez reports that local authorities in Yakima, Washington, have noticed an increase in the number of girls in gangs. The authorities point out that women in gangs often have to play the roles of both feminine girlfriends and tough street fighters. A probation officer named Michael Fairbanks notes that though women may have different roles from men in gangs, they are becoming more aggressive and similar to men. Eloisa Ruano Gonzalez is a staff writer at the Orlando Sentinel, *in Orlando, Florida.*

As you read, consider the following questions:

1. In what ways are women unequal to men in gangs, according to this viewpoint?

Eloisa Ruano Gonzalez, "Girls in Gangs; Yakima Authorities See More Female Membership," *The Associated Press State and Local Wire*, June 4, 2007. Reproduced by permission.

2. According to one researcher, what type of crimes are girl gang members most likely to be victims of?

3. According to this viewpoint, are there female gangs that are completely disassociated from male gangs?

Maria Ball is as tough as any man.

But as one of the few girls in the male-dominated Chicanos Por Vida (CPV) Chicanos for Life gang, the 17-year-old Yakima [Washington] resident has a lot to prove.

Hidden under her short boylike haircut, tattoos, body piercings and baggy brown clothing, Ball says she was ready to take punches and bullets to demonstrate her loyalty for CPV and her toughness, just like the men.

"Girls want to prove we can do everything guys can," Ball says. "And sometimes even better."

When Ball joined the gang nearly five years ago [2002], she says, there were only two other girls. So she was initiated, or "jumped in," like the men taking beatings from six guys.

Changes in Women's Involvement

However, Yakima gangs and women's involvement have changed within the last few years. As women in society juggle the roles of wives, mothers and professionals, female gangsters wear the hats of attractive, submissive girlfriends while being violent members. And just like in the work force, girls in gangs get fewer benefits, credibility and recognition for doing the same work as the men.

Mike Fairbanks, a Yakima County juvenile probation officer who works out of Sunnyside [a town in south-central Washington] and oversees many gang members who've gone through the detention center, notices more girls have been recruited lately. He knows that older gang members are racking them up through their younger siblings or watching for potential newbies outside elementary, middle and high schools.

And many girls join gangs because their boyfriends are involved in them, he adds, while others seek them for drugs, friends and a sense of belonging.

Fairbanks says he monitors eight gang-related girls, 16 percent of his 50-person load. But he expects the numbers to increase within the next few years.

Although Yakima Valley officers are seeing a spike in gang involvement by females, Jody Miller, an assistant criminology professor at the University of Missouri-St. Louis, doesn't expect any drastic changes nationwide.

Miller, who's researched girls in gangs for more than a decade and written several books on gangs, says nothing indicates there was or will be an increase although numbers on previous decades are hard to come by. She says girls and young women have been in gangs since the early 1900s. Scholars just never paid any attention to them until the 1990s, when gang activity in the United States was on the rise.

Miller believes the lack of earlier information makes it difficult to track any nationwide changes including increases.

"If police aren't paying attention to females, they're not going to show up (in reports)," she explains.

Female Gangsters Are Becoming More Aggressive

Fairbanks, who has worked in Sunnyside's detention center for six years, pays attention, though.

He notices the juvenile detention center sees more girls taking part in more violent fights in Yakima County against other girls and men. He says the girls have been more aggressive, causing their roles to shift.

Ball, who hasn't been active in the gang since her best friend [from the gang] Sureno was killed by a rival [from the gang] Norteno, says girls are no longer just attractive "walking billboards" sporting gang colors. She says their roles have

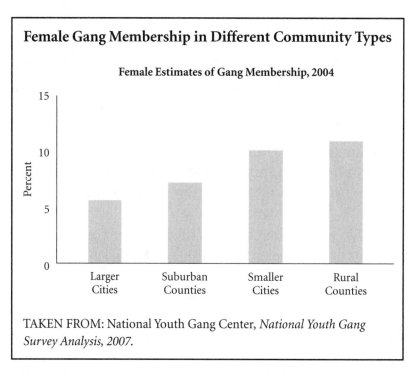

Female Gang Membership in Different Community Types

Female Estimates of Gang Membership, 2004

TAKEN FROM: National Youth Gang Center, *National Youth Gang Survey Analysis, 2007.*

changed within the past few years, requiring them to take part in rumbles and crimes, including stealing beer, carrying guns and shooting at people.

Fairbanks says they often help the men set up the locations for fights and hold their weapons. And he's seen girls arrested for petty crimes such as car prowls, shoplifting, low-class thefts and burglaries. They also start their own fights with men and women from rival gangs, he adds.

Arturo Santana, probation officer with the Yakima juvenile courts, says most girls he monitors have been arrested for misdemeanors and low-class felonies, including fourth-degree assault, third-degree theft, minor in possession of alcohol and malicious mischief for graffiti. Although it was more common years ago, Santana says, girls continue to steal "hip" clothing to blanket the men.

Santana says, though, that a female gang member can be just as dangerous as her male counterparts.

However, Miller says most violent crimes in the U.S. including homicides and drive-by shootings are carried out by men, not women. And she doesn't believe that's going to change.

While researching gang homicides from the St. Louis Police Department for nearly 12 years, Miller didn't find any females connected to those crimes in more than 100 cases. She says girls are less likely to be victims of direct crimes, instead becoming victims for being in the wrong place at the wrong time such as getting shot during a drive-by intended for someone else.

Ball's life has played out differently, though.

Several months ago, the CPV member was stabbed in the left shoulder by a rival gang member. She also has been shot several times once in the leg, once in the rib and twice in the back.

But Ball says rival gang members often don't know she's a girl because she doesn't look like one. She says the males often see her as just another guy, particularly because she also dates women.

"They treated me like any other guy because of the way I acted," she says.

However, not all girls get the same treatment as the men.

The Effects of Machismo

Miller says girls often don't get respect because most gangs are male-dominated and emphasize machismo, aggressive masculine pride as it's done on the streets.

That attitude isn't much different on Yakima Valley streets.

Detective Jim Ortiz of the Sunnyside Police Department says the girls will never be seen as equals, although their roles and physical abilities are similar.

Instead, he finds girls being treated as "go-betweens," keeping an eye on rival gang activity and setting up fights. Ortiz also says some girls are given the option of being "sexed in" requiring them to have sex with numerous members, using protection or not, depending on the gang.

Besides risking sexually transmitted diseases, Miller says, the girls face other difficulties when choosing to be "sexed in." She says girls face further sexual abuse after gaining a promiscuous reputation, losing respect from both genders.

Miller doubts the machismo attitude will change anytime soon.

"We haven't been able to achieve that in society as a whole," she notes. "Why would we expect gangs to be that (equal)?"

Exclusively Female Gangs

Ball says some female members are branching into their own group to try to become more independent. However, they're still affiliated with the male-dominant gang.

In Yakima, Ball knows of a few female groups. They include the Play Gift Surenas, affiliated with the Surenos; Varrio Rojas Carnalitas, affiliated with Varrio Campo Vida; La Krazy Criminals, affiliated with North Side Villains; and the red-rival Crazy Girl Nortenas. With more girls in them, they're responsible for jumping in new members, the violent initiation rite Ball underwent when she joined, which shows they have the same aggression as men.

Fairbanks isn't surprised.

"They're trying to reach their own level of exposure," he explains.

Fairbanks says girls have been trying to split from male-dominated gangs because they don't want to be "somebody else's puppet."

However, Miller says it's uncommon to see girls become fully detached from the males. Only about 10 percent of gangs throughout the country are exclusively made up of females and have no allegiance to a male-dominated group.

"It has to do with how gender operates in the street world," she says.

It's a world Ball no longer wants to be a part of, particularly after losing her friend to that shooting more than a year ago. Although her family, including her brother and cousins, have been involved in gangs for generations, she doesn't want to end up like her friend.

"I grew up gang-affiliated since I was little," Ball explains. "But other things got more important. Hey, I don't want to die over a color."

But she says she doesn't see a way out of Chicanos Por Vida except in a casket.

"There's no other choice," she laments.

> "This week's horror stories about girl gangs ... are strikingly short on hard evidence but long on hair-raising interviews with kids who claim to have personal experience of the phenomenon."

The Problem of Girl Gangs Has Been Exaggerated

Joan Smith

In the following viewpoint, Joan Smith questions the claim that there are a growing number of girl gangs in London; she feels girl gang participation has been exaggerated and sensationalized in the media, noting that news reports involving girl gangs usually are based on anecdotes about crimes involving female gang members, but provide no clear statistics. She also writes that growing paranoia over girl gangs both glamorizes gangs and alienates youth. Joan Smith is a columnist, critic, novelist, and human rights activist who often writes about atheism and feminism.

As you read, consider the following questions:

1. What phenomenon does the author describe as "one of the iron rules of a misogynistic culture"?

Joan Smith, "Are Devil Girls Really on the Rampage?" *The Independent*, August 23, 2007, p. 34. Reproduced by permission.

2. How many female gangs are there in London, according to the Metropolitan Police?

3. What distinction needs to be made when discussing gangs, according to the Youth Justice Board?

It's a bit like watching the trailer for that hilarious sci-fi classic, Attack of the 50 Ft Woman, which thrilled audiences with the news that "the most grotesque monstrosity of all" was on the loose. This time, to be fair, the monsters are the same size as the rest of us but the really terrible thing about them, like the deranged avenger in that Fifties movie, is their sex.

"Girls are killing guys", a young man declared on yesterday morning's Today programme. "They think girls are angels and boys are devils, but sometimes girls can be the devil", said a terrified 14-year-old girl.

Ah, those devil girls: it could only be August, a month when killer sharks are spotted off Cornwall, baby tigers pop through cat flaps and David Cameron [a member of Parliament in the United Kingdom] promises to repeal the Human Rights Act. To be honest, I'm kicking myself; when last week's big news story was the danger of confronting teenage boys about their anti-social behaviour, I should have known that "bad girls"—as Jenni Murray memorably called them on [British radio program] Woman's Hour a couple of months ago [June 2007]—would not be far behind. It's happened so often that on this occasion I can't even be bothered to misquote [Victorian novelist Rudyard] Kipling on the female of the species being deadlier than the male.

Is This a Case of Misogyny?

It's one of the iron rules of a misogynistic culture that any story about men or boys behaving badly has to be followed by a "balancing" piece in which someone points out that women and girls are pretty awful too. This is not to suggest I don't think there's a problem with adolescent boys and anti-social behaviour, . . . but it's important to keep things in proportion; not every boy aged between 13 and 18 is in a gang, carrying a knife or gun and looking for a confrontation to prove how tough he is.

The number of young men injured and killed in this kind of violence is unacceptable but the solution—teaching vulnerable boys to have a secure identity which isn't based on violence—is pretty obvious. At the same time, as long as this kind of brittle, showy masculinity continues to be valorised in popular culture—and it certainly is in rap music—it's inevitable that some equally vulnerable girls will be drawn towards it.

Common sense dictates that they will be abused as a result, both sexually—being raped by gang members is not uncommon—and by being lured into criminal behaviour themselves.

It is a fact that men commit many more violent offences than women, although violent women—because they offend cultural notions about women being the "nurturing" sex—tend to get heavier sentences; when taboos are broken, people are horrified and excited in about equal measure, something that's worth bearing in mind whenever the subject of female violence returns to the agenda.

The Lack of Strong Evidence

This week's [August 2007] horror stories about girl gangs are a perfect example; they are strikingly short on hard evidence but long on hair-raising interviews with kids who claim to have personal experience of the phenomenon. "I can show you six or seven [girl gangs] in one area", claimed an excitable interviewee on yesterday's Today programme.

This would suggest that London has dozens, if not hundreds, of girl gangs rampaging through the streets and causing mayhem. Yet the Metropolitan Police is aware of a total of 170

Some Statistics on Girls and Violence

- While girl gang violence may be prominent in the public's imagination, the reality is, as a recent Elizabeth Fry Society report reveals, that only 3.83% of violent crimes are committed by young female offenders.

- Women's struggle for equality has not yet been realized and is certainly not reflected in the lifestyles or behaviour of women who use violence. Women who use violence are marginalized and have usually suffered a history of abuse and likely emulate their abusers and abuse themselves.

- In 88% of all violent incidents males are identified as the suspects; half of all incidents involve a male perpetrator and a female victim.

- Working Groups on Girls (WGGs) noted in its report that immigrant and refugee girls also experience higher rates of violence because of dislocation, racism, and sexism from both within their own communities and the external society.

"Girls and Violence: Some Statistics,"
The FREDA Centre for Research on Violence Against
Women and Children, Simon Fraser University, Vancouver.

gangs in the capital and, of those, only three are exclusively female. This hasn't stopped the BBC [British Broadcasting Corporation] returning to the subject throughout the summer, with Woman's Hour and a Radio 1 documentary entitled Mean Girls blazing the trail for yesterday's Today investigation. "Shock! Frenzy! Devastation!" Sorry, I'm talking about Attack of the 50 Ft Woman again, although there's clearly no shortage of kids in 2007 who are willing to tell reporters about muggings and robberies they have witnessed or taken part in.

Such claims are impossible to verify, especially when the interviewees are identified only by a first name; some of them sound very much like teenage bragging. What is needed to justify all these colourful claims is some statistics, and they have been noticeably absent. "A BBC investigation for the Today programme has found that an increasing number of girls are operating in gangs, some as young as seven", James Naughtie declared yesterday, yet the report which followed offered no hard evidence for the proposition. Naughtie suggested that girl gangs are "prevalent", which certainly doesn't match my experience.

Two months earlier, there was a surreal discussion on Woman's Hour which simply assumed that girl gangs were a growing problem. Jenni Murray, usually the most sensible of interviewers, asked how this situation had come about and what should be done without ever establishing that the problem really existed.

The item was prompted by a real event, the fatal stabbing of a girl in Croydon a week earlier which was said to have followed an argument between the victim and a girl gang, and the programme claimed there had been "an increase in reported incidents of girls' involvement in gang violence".

Once again, this is an imprecise formulation which could mean one of several things—that more girls are being drawn into boys' gangs, as girfriends for instance, or that there has been an increase in girls forming their own gangs.

The Need to Get the Story Straight

Susannah Hancock, London regional manager of the Youth Justice Board [part of Britain's Ministry of Justice], thought the first explanation was more likely, telling Murray that boys' gangs were getting younger and that more girls were becoming involved on the periphery—to carry drugs, for instance. She emphasised the danger of classifying any identifiable group of girls as a gang, a point which shouldn't need making given the propensity of girls down the ages to form close friendship groups without necessarily involving themselves in anything worse than sharing lipstick.

Three months ago, the Youth Justice Board addressed the subject of young people's involvement in gangs and stressed the importance of making a distinction between "real" gangs and groups of young people who may commit low-level anti-social behaviour. "Mislabelling of youth groups as gangs runs the risk of glamourising them and may even encourage young people to become involved in more serious criminal behaviour," it warned.

This is a real danger, and one of the few sensible observations that's been made about the subject in recent months.

Another danger is that we start seeing "gangs" on every corner, further alienating kids who are suspicious of adults but haven't yet got involved in criminal behaviour. I'm still no wiser about the number of girls involved in gangs, but you'll have to excuse me while I check my windows—I just can't stop thinking about that 50-foot woman.

"Violence plus the lack of resources and dearth of opportunity made it easy for me and other kids to pursue fantasy lives—to emulate gangster lifestyles and drug dealing."

Gangs Are a Problem of the Underprivileged

Ely Flores

In the following viewpoint, Ely Flores explains to Congress how as a child of a single mother growing up poor in south-central Los Angeles he inevitably fell into a life of violence and gangs. He argues that there are many underprivileged children like him who have no choice but to join a gang, get involved with drugs, and possibly go to prison or be killed. Ely Flores has worked for years in the field of community organizing, youth development, leadership development and organizational training and facilitation.

As you read, consider the following questions:

1. Why did the author's skateboarding friend join a gang?

Ely Flores, "Addressing Gang Violence," Testimony of Ely Flores before the Subcommittee on Crime, Terrorism, and Homeland Security Membership, June 10, 2008. Reproduced by permission of the author.

2. Who else besides individuals must be held accountable for the cycle of violence that includes gangs, according to the author?

3. Why weren't rehabilitation programs in jails helpful to the author?

As a child, I was abandoned by my father and I grew up in both south Hollywood and South Central L.A. [Los Angeles]—in a under resourced, oppressed community where more youth are sent to prisons rather than rehabilitation programs. Our mothers were so overwhelmed they could do little to prevent us young men from searching for meaning and a sense of belonging on streets that led straight to prison or death. Violence was my learned resolution for all the challenges I faced. Like many young people who grow up in poor, disenfranchised communities with few opportunities, I lived by the law of "dog eat dog" and "survival of the fittest."

A Life of Violence

I raised my fists in violence over nothing. Maybe someone made fun of my shoes or clothes. Perhaps someone talked negatively about my mother, brother, or sister. Perhaps someone challenged my so called "man hood." A fight was always the conclusion. Where I'm from, being scarred and bruised was like wearing military stripes or medals won on a battlefield. Whenever the pain was too much to bear, a dose of marijuana relieved me. The older gangsters found it fun to pit a kid against another kid by instigating little disagreements that escalated into a fight. Violence was commonplace. It was entertainment and to us kids, it seemed normal.

Violence plus the lack of resources and dearth of opportunity made it easy for me and other kids to pursue fantasy lives—to emulate gangster lifestyles and drug dealing. My brother and I slipped into that, too. I've been in situations where I was forced to fight individuals for "claiming" (stating) their membership to another gang that we did not get along with. My anger and violence led me to use weapons; to hurt people. I conditioned myself not to care whether or not my victim ended up in the hospital or dead. The same rules my homies and I lived by, also ruled the people I thought of as my enemy.

One of the experiences that changed my life was when one of my homies was shot dead at the age of 14. He used to be a skate boarder. He always promised that he'd never join a gang. But one day peer pressure—and a lack of other options—got the best of him. He joined the local gang. A month later he was shot and killed next to my grandmother's house. The cycle continued with years of retaliation. Life stories like mine are quite common amongst poor and disenfranchised youth everywhere in the U.S. First we begin to hang out with gangs and eventually this road takes us to places like prison, drug addiction, and homelessness and for some of us, death.

A Different Way of Thinking

As I began developing my consciousness about social issues, I asked myself, "Why are there so many poor people in prisons and especially black and brown people? And why do they keep going back? Is it the people's fault, the community's fault, or the parents?" Then I realized that I was trying to come up with answers from an oppressed and deficit perspective. Of course there has to be some accountability for the people but accountability also must lie with institutions that contribute to the problem and don't help to solve this problem that [affects] not just the young people caught up in a cycle of violence and deprivation, but the entire society in which we live.

South Central L.A. is already a poor community but continuously prisons (in the absence of decent educational programs and rehabilitation programs) and police continue the criminalization of many communities of color. I agree that there needs to be law enforcement and too, incarceration for

Juvenile Poverty and Juvenile Crime

Research has often found a connection between poverty and self-reported delinquency. For example, [researcher David P.] Farrington found that low family income measured when the youth was age 8 predicted self-reported violence in the teenage years and conviction rates for violent offenses. Research, however, indicates that the linkage may not be direct. For example, [researcher Robert J.] Sampson found that poverty exerts much influence on family disruption (e.g., marital separation, divorce), which in turn has a direct influence on juvenile violent crime rates. He also found that family disruption had a stronger influence on juvenile violence than adult violence. Therefore, differential poverty levels are likely to influence juvenile crime trends.

Howard N. Snyer and Melissa Sickmund,
Juvenile Offenders and Victims: 2006 National Report,
National Center for Juvenile Justice.

the extreme and very few cases of people who might be beyond rehabilitation and who pose a threat to public safety.

But I also believe that there needs to be far more resources, programs, jobs and rehabilitation coming to the community, rather than easy arrests, more incarceration, and the costly practice of just building of more prisons. Too many lives, especially those of young people of color, are just being written off in a society that pours its vital resources into imprisoning a most precious resource: Young people who are truly eager to contribute in a positive manner to something meaningful, other than to gang fights on the street. As I adopted a gang life style, incarceration naturally followed. For four years I went in and out of prison. Some people say I was just a knuckle head but I say that the mission statements of jails that claim to rehabilitate people skipped me. I was never given any resources to better my life or to improve a community I truly did care for. I had to go hunt for resources outside of my community because there simply were not any in mine. I was hungry for change. However, jail and probation officers never seemed to believe me. I felt I'd been written off. But, I was lucky in the end. I found an organization like the Youth Justice Coalition and LA CAUSA [Los Angeles Communities Advocating for Unity, Social Justice, and Action] YouthBuild that believe in the empowerment of young people to better their lives and their communities.

The Benefit of LA CAUSA YouthBuild

LA CAUSA YouthBuild, an affiliate of YouthBuild USA, and a grantee of the US Department of Labor's YouthBuild program, introduced me to a life of positive transformation, self accountability, and leadership. It is but one example—a successful example—of what's possible when government resources are invested in young people rather than in jails that warehouse them. This organization offered me the opportunity to develop lifelong skills that would better myself and most important, would allow me to be a part of something bigger than myself. YouthBuild allowed me the privilege of contributing in a positive manner to my community. I participated full-time and earned my GED [General Educational Development, a high school equivalency certificate]. At the same time, I learned priceless job skills while building much-needed affordable housing for homeless and low income people. All the while, YouthBuild staff provided personal counseling and positive role models, a safe environment. I learned leadership skills and received encouragement from the staff members, who unlike the employees of the jails I was in, really believed in me. This wasn't a welfare program. YouthBuild provided the key. It was up to me to open that door to a new road. Getting on this road forever changed my life.

Because of that key they offered me, I became an activist. Because of that key, I have developed a passion for community work and helped numerous people in diverse and challenging communities. That opportunity that is rarely given to people was given to me and has enabled me to become an expert in the field of Youth Development, Leadership Development, and Community Organizing and has allowed me to train others across this nation. That opportunity and handing of resources has given me congressional recognition by [California congresswoman] Hilda Solis and recognition from the city of Los Angeles. That recognition has even given me the opportunity to fly to Israel and devote my time to try and build peace amongst Israeli and Palestinian Youth. Imagine that. An ex-gang member, a once violent young man, a former drug addict and ex-criminal now offers his life and time to serve for the cause of peace and the people. Yes, I worked hard to get where I am. But my story is not an anomaly. So many young people, given a chance through well-designed, positive youth programs, really can turn their lives around and contribute in positive ways to make communities safer and more prosperous.

The Necessity of This Program

I want you to imagine for a minute that I, Ely Flores of Los Angeles, CA, the person that stands in front of you today, was never given that key for transformation. What would have I become? A long term prisoner, a wanted felon or just another city and national statistic of incarcerated people of color. Your guess is as good as mine. But that key was given to me by a group of people of color who looked like me, who created an organization that offered me resources and empowerment in East Los Angeles and deterred my direction of destruction towards a direction of productivity. The resources to give me that key came from the federal government, thanks to decisions of legislators like you, who decided to fund the federal YouthBuild program. The problem is, that the 226 YouthBuild programs that have been created with federal funds and serve just 8,000 youth a year are turning away many thousands of young people like me every year for lack of funds, and 1,000 organizations have applied to the federal government for YouthBuild funding and most have been turned away for lack of funds. This is a sin and a tragedy, as I think of the young people coming behind me who will not have the opportunity I have had. Right now [2008], there is a recommendation in front of the appropriations sub-committee for Labor/HHS [Department of Health and Human Services] from many legislators and the Congressional Black Caucus and the Latino Caucus and the US Conference of Mayors to increase the YouthBuild appropriation from $59M [million] to $100M, and I fervently hope they will do it.

I urge you all to become heroic politicians and people that offer keys of transformation to the thousands of youth and adults with a potential like mine—the potential to become agents for change to their communities and the future of this nation. Think about my story and use it as proof that change is possible in communities dominated by the gang culture if you just provide and offer well-designed and well-managed resources and opportunities to communities in poverty. At the very least, equalize resources and opportunities to those of the rising prison systems. Be the givers of those keys that will open thousands of doors of hope, doors of transformation, and doors of change to people like me. Make the right choice. Choose hope and optimism.

I thank you for your time. I ask only that you keep in mind the possibility that a young gang member can become a productive member of society. It is possible for a gang member to become an agent for positive change.

Thank you for the opportunity to testify on this very important matter.

"*[The gang] soon shifted its base to nearby Orange County and in the 1990s began recruiting what police call "bored latchkey kids" . . . from upper-middle class neighborhoods.*"

Privileged Children Also Get Involved in Gangs

Gillian Flaccus

In the following viewpoint, Gillian Flaccus describes the origins, growth and activities of the white supremacist gang, Public Enemy No. 1. She explains that this gang started among upper middle class teenagers in southern California and is involved in gun and drug sales as well as identity theft. Gillian Flaccus is the diversity and religion reporter for southern California, for The Associated Press.

As you read, consider the following questions:

1. What, according to the article, is a sign of how bold Public Enemy No. 1 has become?

2. What has increased Public Enemy No. 1's wealth and recruiting power?

3. Where and when, according to the author, did Public Enemy No. 1 start?

The white supremacist gang Public Enemy No. 1 began two decades ago as a group of teenage punk-rock fans from upper-middle class bedroom communities in Southern California.

Now, the violent gang that deals in drugs, guns and identity theft is gaining clout across the West after forging an alliance with the notorious Aryan Brotherhood, authorities say.

Police say the gang has compiled a "hit list" targeting five officers and a gang prosecutor, a sign of just how brazen Public Enemy has become.

"They make police officers very, very nervous," said ... Nate Booth, a gang detective with the Buena Park Police Department in Orange County.

Public Enemy No. 1 and the Aryan Brotherhood

Law enforcement officials trace the gang's rise to shifts in the power structure inside prisons.

The Aryan Brotherhood has long been the dominant white supremacist gang behind bars, with the Nazi Low Riders acting as its foot soldiers on the outside for drug dealing and identity theft.

In 2000, officials reclassified the Low Riders as a prison-based gang and began sending its members to solitary confinement as soon as they were imprisoned.

The crackdown hurt the gang's ability to interact with the Aryan Brotherhood, which turned to Public Enemy, authorities say. The alliance was cemented in 2005 when Donald Reed "Popeye" Mazza, an alleged leader of Public Enemy, was inducted into the Aryan Brotherhood.

The pact has increased Public Enemy's wealth and recruiting power, said Steve Slaten, a special agent for the California Department of Corrections.

Gangs and the Middle Class

That 15% of gang members may be from the middle- and upper-middle class is supported by my observations in the field and suggests probation/parole and police officers are correct when they say "Gang members can be found in all neighborhoods, rich or poor."

Mike Carlie, Into the Abyss:
A Personal Journey into the World of Street Gangs, *2002.*

In the past three years [2004–2007], its ranks have doubled to at least 400, but authorities suspect there could be hundreds of other members operating under the radar. They said heavy recruiting is taking place throughout California and Arizona, and members have been picked up by police in Nevada and Idaho.

"They move around. We find them everywhere," said Lowell Smith of the Orange County Probation Department.

The Origin and Activities of the Gang

The gang traces its roots to the punk rock subculture in Long Beach in the 1980s. It soon shifted its base to nearby Orange County and in the 1990s began recruiting what police call "bored latchkey kids"—white teenagers from upper-middle class neighborhoods.

Public Enemy is now involved in identity theft. Booth said the gang has gone from swiping personal information from mailboxes and trash to stealing entire credit profiles with the help of girlfriends and wives who take jobs at banks, mortgage companies and even state motor vehicle departments.

Money from those operations is used to fuel its methamphetamine business, he said.

Two months ago, police agencies in Orange County arrested 67 suspected members after learning about the hit list against officers in Anaheim, Buena Park and Costa Mesa. Those arrested in the raid were charged with conspiracy to commit murder, possession of illegal weapons and identity theft, among other things. Police have not released their names or further details because the investigation is continuing.

Booth recalled another case in which a member of the gang fired dozens of rounds at police from a car driven by his girlfriend during a high-speed freeway pursuit. After being arrested, the man was taken to an emergency room, where he grabbed a scalpel and tried to slash a deputy before cutting himself, Booth said.

Authorities worry that Public Enemy is using stolen credit information to learn the home addresses of police and their families. Some officers have gone to court to have addresses removed from those records, Booth said.

> "The gang took root in Los Angeles in the early 1980s as waves of Salvadorans fleeing civil war in their homeland arrived there, said Susan Ritter, head of the Department of Criminal Justice at the University of Texas at Brownsville, who has studied MS-13."

Immigration Contributes to the Gang Problem

Brian R. Ballou and Maria Sacchetti

In the following viewpoint, the authors describe raids by the Immigration and Customs Enforcement agency in Massachusetts in August of 2007. The raids were believed to have targeted members of the Salvadoran gang MS-13. Susan Ritter, head of the Department of Criminal Justice at the University of Texas at Brownsville, explains how the gang formed when refugees fleeing El Salvador came to the United States. Brian R. Ballou and Maria Sacchetti are staff reporters for The Boston Globe.

As you read, consider the following questions:

1. Why did the raids cause panic among some immigrants?

Brian R. Ballou and Maria Sacchetti, "Immigration Raids Target Violent Gang: Crimes Spur Sweep in Three cities," *The Boston Globe*, August 29, 2007, p. A1. Copyright © 2007 Globe Newspaper Company. All rights reserved. Reproduced by permission.

2. Why was this sweep by Customs officials assumed to be part of an antigang crackdown?

3. Why, according to Susan Ritter, did some Salvadorans coming to the U.S. form a gang?

Federal agents and local police swept into Chelsea, Somerville, and East Boston [Massachusetts] yesterday in an attempt to arrest dozens of suspects, some believed to be members of a violent Salvadoran gang, on outstanding warrants.

The sweep, dubbed Operation 13, had been in the planning stages for weeks in response to crimes perpetrated by the MS-13 [Mara Salvatrucha] gang, said Chelsea police Captain Brian Kyes. He said the operation targeted up to 50 people and was headed by the Immigration and Customs Enforcement agency and included officials from the Bureau of Alcohol, Tobacco, Firearms, and Explosives; the Middlesex Sheriff's Department; police from the Massachusetts Bay Transportation Authority [MBTA]; and local police departments.

Authorities Do Not Explain Raids

Immigration advocates said families in Lynn, Revere, and Everett also reported arrests, but authorities in those cities would not confirm the accounts. The suspects in the raids were sought on weapons charges and for violent offenses.

Customs spokesman Michael Gilhooly confirmed the raids took place, but would not say how many people were arrested or where they were being held. Similar sweeps against MS-13 have taken place recently in Chicago, Omaha, and other cities.

As the law enforcement officials knocked on doors yesterday morning, panic spread among immigrants, apparently in fear that they would be swept up in another crackdown on undocumented workers. Some said they remained indoors because of the raids.

But federal officials were looking for specific people, Gilhooly said. "We don't do random operations. We are targeting specific individuals who are a threat to public safety."

The sweep unfolded on the same day as the local launch of a federal program that illuminates a different aspect of the government's immigration strategy. Alfonso Aguilar, chief of the US Office of Citizenship, unveiled a new effort at Boston's City Hall to encourage legal immigrants and US citizens to volunteer in their communities, learn English and American civics, and assimilate.

Customs would not confirm reports that yesterday's [August 28, 2007] arrests were part of an antigang crackdown, but in 2005 the agency launched Operation Community Shield, a national effort targeting MS-13. Since then, federal authorities have expanded the operation to include all gangs, leading to the arrests of more than 4,800 alleged members of about 350 gangs across the country, according to the agency's website.

Some of the suspects being sought yesterday may have slipped through the net.

While federal authorities would not say how many immigrants they were seeking, MBTA Deputy Chief Paul Mac-Millan said a transit officer was part of a small group of law enforcement officials who scoured East Boston. "They came up empty after going to three houses," he said. "They couldn't find who they were looking for."

Relatives and co-workers of two of those detained described the operation as quick and efficient.

Rumors Cause Panic Among Immigrant Workers

An East Boston man who identified himself only as Eric said that immigration officials entered his brother's apartment yesterday morning with a warrant for a man who no longer lived in the building. The agents arrested his brother, a permanent resident and native of El Salvador, after they discovered that he had been convicted of a minor alcohol-related felony three years ago [2004].

Illegal Immigration and Gangs

[William Gheen]: "MS-13 and other illegal immigrant gangs are bringing in the illegals, drugs, heavy weapons, and possibly terrorists. The biggest threat from their members is contained in the multiple intelligence reports provided to Congress indicating that Al-Qaeda and MS-13 are now working together to smuggle terrorist operatives and materials into the U.S. Equally daunting is the fact that illegal aliens in America already live under Gang Rule, and if Central and South America provide a sound example, so will the rest of us when these gangs reach higher strength levels. In Mexico, citizens do not call the police when their children are stolen by the gangs. They live under Gang Rule, and a call to police over a stolen child can result in executions."

Sher Zieve interviewing William Gheen,
Post Chronicle, *October 22, 2005.*

"He's a hard worker," Eric said. "He's not a gang member. It was his bad luck that he was there." He said immigration officials are holding his brother at a federal building in downtown Boston, but he had no word on how long he would be detained.

In Somerville, immigration agents entered the A Plus Auto Body shop on Medford Street and arrested one man bearing a tattoo associated with MS-13, co-workers said. The manager of the shop, Tony Fragione, said that the man, who told his co-workers his name was Henry Morales, was one of the store's best employees.

"He worked all available hours," Fragione said. "He was a really nice kid. I feel bad for him."

The operation paralyzed parts of East Boston, Chelsea, and Somerville. A day-labor stand in Somerville, typically bustling with painters and dry-wallers, stood nearly empty at 9:30 a.m. Callers flooded a Spanish language talk-radio show with sightings or rumors of green-uniformed customs agents in their neighborhoods.

In East Boston, people said there was an eerie calm in banks and stores in Maverick Square.

"The streets of East Boston were barren," said Gail Viola, an employee of Sterlingwear of Boston, who visited a bank in the neighborhood around 10 a.m.

"People are scared," said Yessenia Alfaro, a community organizer at the Chelsea Collaborative, which received nearly 20 phone calls about the raid yesterday. "They don't know what's going on. They don't want to go out of their houses. It's just terrifying."

Rumors ran wild, sending some people into hiding. A Lynn man said immigration agents were at a local supermarket.

At Sterlingwear, a factory that makes wool peacoats and other gear for the US Navy, workers abruptly stopped cutting and sewing when WUNR 1600 AM reportedly broadcast, incorrectly, that immigration agents were on their way.

Workers frantically searched their pockets and purses for ID cards, said Jack Foster, director of marketing and sales. About a dozen of the 120 employees had forgotten their papers and went home to get them, he said.

"It's created a major panic here for no reason," said Foster, who said all workers had legal documents. "We were just dumbfounded by the whole thing."

MS-13 in the United States

The crackdown reflected concerns among law enforcement officials that MS-13 may be growing in New England.

The gang took root in Los Angeles in the early 1980s as waves of Salvadorans fleeing civil war in their homeland arrived there, said Susan Ritter, head of the Department of Criminal Justice at the University of Texas at Brownsville, who has studied MS-13.

Some of the refugees formed a gang, the Mara Salvatrucha, for protection after being repeatedly victimized by Hispanic gangs in Los Angeles, Ritter said. Trained by former Salvadoran guerrillas, the gang members became known for their vicious attacks and attracted members from elsewhere in Central America.

Members soon migrated to cities with significant pockets of Salvadorans or other Hispanics: Washington, D.C., Houston, New York, Detroit, and eventually Boston. The gang deals mostly in drugs, arms, and car theft.

Ritter said the gang's presence in the Boston [area] is lower key than in other cities. "Maybe they're just getting started," she said.

"Some equally outlandish theories about immigrants and crime bit the dust when a leaked police report concluded that the 800,000 or so east Europeans who have arrived since 2004 are neither more nor less likely to commit crimes than the rest of the population."

Immigrants Are Not Responsible for Increases in Criminal Activity

The Economist

In the following viewpoint, the author discredits some commonly held misconceptions about immigrants and crime in Great Britain, claiming that immigrants are not more likely to commit crimes than natives. Furthermore, according to this viewpoint, the victims of crimes committed by immigrants are usually themselves immigrants which means that immigrant crime does not adversely effect Great Britain's natives. The Economist *is a news journal based in Great Britain.*

"Not Guilty: Migrants are Mostly Law-abiding, but the Police Need More Cash to Do Their Job," *The Economist*, April 17, 2008. Republished with permission of *The Economist*, conveyed through Copyright Clearance Center, Inc.

As you read, consider the following questions:

1. Why are total crime levels increasing in Britain, according to this viewpoint?

2. What percentage of prisoners in Britain are foreigners?

3. What, according to this viewpoint, seems to be true about European countries with a large proportion of foreign prisoners?

Immigrants, long the focus of much excitement in Britain, are turning out to be a reassuringly boring bunch. Wild theories about their economic impact (miraculous, according to the government; disastrous, according to detractors) were flattened earlier this month [April 2008] by a sober report from the House of Lords [a branch of the United Kingdom's Parliament], which found that high levels of net migration over the past decade have had "very small impacts" on Britons' personal incomes. On April 16th [2008] some equally outlandish theories about immigrants and crime bit the dust when a leaked police report concluded that the 800,000 or so east Europeans who have arrived since 2004 are neither more nor less likely to commit crimes than the rest of the population, as some had claimed.

Unpacking Crime Statistics

All those extra people mean that total crime is higher than it would otherwise be, but the increase in crime per capita is negligible. (Mischievously, the government likes to tell this story the other way around when it promotes the economic benefits of immigration.) In the case of crimes that are disproportionately committed by migrants, the impact on everyone else is often slight because they share the burden of victimhood as well. Take homicide: in the year to April 2007, a third of those charged with the offence in London were foreigners—but a third of identified victims were foreign, too.

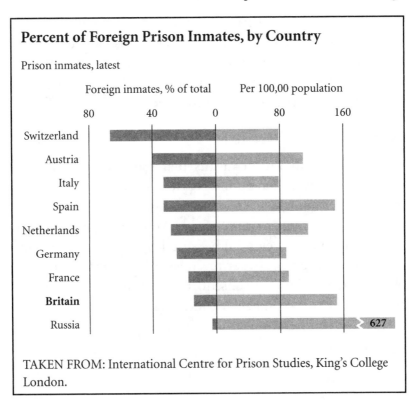

Percent of Foreign Prison Inmates, by Country

Prison inmates, latest

TAKEN FROM: International Centre for Prison Studies, King's College London.

The police report unearthed some interesting trends among the newest arrivals. Poles are bad about driving under the influence of drink, for instance. More seriously, it linked east Europeans to people-trafficking. And some other cases stick in the mind: on April 1st [2008] two young children opened a plastic bag on a Scottish beach to discover the severed head of a Lithuanian woman. Two Lithuanian men have since been charged with her murder. Police would rather not see any more of the criminal gangs that blight the Balkans.

It could be much worse. In Britain's prisons, just 14% of inmates are foreign nationals—low compared with most big European countries (see chart). Foreigners take up less than half as much of Britain's jail space as they do of Italy's, for example, despite making up a bigger share of the general population. Are Britain's immigrants a better behaved crowd? Are the police less racist? Perhaps neither: a third explanation is that countries with a big share of foreign prisoners tend to be those with low overall levels of imprisonment—so it may be more accurate to say that Britain locks up a lot of natives than to assert that it imprisons few foreigners.

More Police Are Needed

Either way, immigration means that the police need more money, like any other public service. This should not be a problem: because they tend to be employed, east Europeans pay their way in taxes. Maddeningly, however, some towns do not get the money they need because Britain's centralised government sucks up most tax revenues and doesn't always distribute them fairly. One consequence is strained policing, and an easier ride for criminals. Crime might be up in some areas because of immigration—but the migrants themselves have been framed.

Periodical Bibliography

The following articles have been selected to supplement the diverse views presented in this chapter.

Bryan Appleyard — "Hanging Out with the Ghetto's Gordon Gekkos," *The Sunday Times (London)*, February 17, 2008.

Simon Black — "Targeting T.O.'s Street Gangs: No Matter How Much Money the Police Spend on Enforcement, Gangs Are Not Going Away," *Toronto Star*, July 2, 2008.

Martyn Brown — "Scandal of Britain's Romanian Gangsters: Crime by Migrants Soars 530%," *The Express*, January 25, 2008.

Sherry Chiu — "New Chinatown Gangs Engage in Nontraditional Crimes," *World Journal*, August 1, 2006.

Marc Lacey — "Abuse Trails Central American Girls into Gangs," *New York Times*, April 11, 2008.

Heather Mac Donald — "Immigration and the Alien Gang Epidemic: Problems and Solutions," Manhattan Institute for Policy Research, April 13, 2005. www.manhattan-institute.org.

Angela Neustatter — "G2: Blood Sisters," *The Guardian*, July 4, 2008.

Gretchen Ruethling — "Chicago Gangs Move to Suburbs, Study Finds," *New York Times*, June 21, 2006.

Jerry Seper — "Spread of Gangs Tied to Border-Control Failure: Transnational Groups Found to be Mobile and Adaptable," *Washington Times*, October 3, 2008.

Jennifer Steinhauer — "Immigration, Gang Violence and a Crusade," *International Herald Tribune*, May 15, 2008.

OPPOSING
VIEWPOINTS®
SERIES

CHAPTER 2

Why Do People Join Gangs?

Chapter Preface

A gang may provide a kind of family support for some children who do not have caring or responsible parents. Many authors emphasize the great importance of parental guidance and parental role models in discouraging children from choosing to turn to gangs.

A parent helps a child to establish a sense of self-worth. Responsible parents keep track of their children's lives, asking them questions which not only help them establish a moral sense but also give children the idea that what they do is important. A child who doesn't have an involved parent may join a gang because the gang supplies this same sense of importance and brotherhood. The *Associated Press* on December 28, 2008, profiled Chris Mulitalo as a man who understands the lure of gangs for local children. Mulitalo works for Youth Impact, a nonprofit organization serving at-risk youths. He explains about the children he works with: "A lot of these kids come from broken homes. A lot of them have no male figure in their lives."

Children may be driven to criminal behavior because their parents don't take responsibility for them. Members of the community who see youths at their worst, when they have become deeply engaged in criminal behavior, still see the lack of a foundation of family support or adult role models as the main reason children turn to gangs. Jerrauld C. Jones, a Virginia district court judge, explains that the children he sees on a daily basis in the juvenile justice system lack parental guidance. "Nothing that I have seen in [27 years of working in the juvenile justice system] has caused me to lose confidence in the belief that children, even those who are highly delinquent and criminalized in their behavior, are in need of the same things that you and I, and I daresay, most everyone else in this room this afternoon, had as children growing up—the love and affection of a caring, responsible adult in their lives. . . . Like us, the children of today need parents and other caring adults who provide not only love, but who also instill the proper discipline, values, morals, and boundaries in the life of a child from birth and beyond."

The media also reflects an attitude that it is a parent's responsibility to show their children they care what they do and thus remove their temptation to join gangs. The *Evening Standard* reported British politician David Cameron as saying, "Parents who don't know where their kids are and what they're up to at night should not just be helped to do their job properly—they should be shamed into doing it . . . [and] fathers who abandon their families, should be treated like the selfish people they are." In the following chapters the authors discuss some of the different reasons children and adults are drawn to gangs.

> *"Young people frequently see gangs as an attractive choice or a solution to their problems."*

Adolescents Join Gangs for a Sense of Social Belonging

Phelan Wyrick

In the following viewpoint, Phelan Wyrick explains that the beginning of adolescence is the most likely time for joining a gang because it is the time when young people are developing their identities. He writes that during this period of identity formation a gang can offer the respect and sense of belonging that all adolescents desire. Phelan Wyrick is the coordinator of a gang prevention program at the Office of Juvenile Justice and Delinquency Prevention.

As you read, consider the following questions:

1. What does the author say is the central developmental challenge of adolescence?
2. What does the author say are the "pulls" of gangs for young people?
3. What are the risk factors that push young people into joining gangs, according to the author?

Phelan Wyrick, "Gang Prevention: How to Make the 'Front End' of Your Anti-Gang Effort Work," *United States Attorneys' Bulletin*, vol. 54, no. 3, May 2006, pp. 52–60. Reproduced by permission.

Most people agree with the basic concept that if young people are prevented from joining gangs or if the violence associated with gangs can be stopped, great strides toward accomplishing shared public safety goals will be made. Agreement on this concept, however, is still a long way from having the will, resources, or ability to implement prevention programs that show results. Some people may be skeptical about the feasibility of effective gang prevention, thus, they do not have the will. A few may think too narrowly about gang prevention and the assets that relate to it, thus, they feel there are no resources. Others may have the will and the resources, but they overlook the best practices in implementing gang prevention and related activities.

Gang Prevention

Gang prevention is challenging work. There have been many advances, however, in knowledge and practice, that greatly increase the ability to be successful. U.S. Attorneys' offices can be highly effective leaders in local anti-gang initiatives that incorporate prevention. Federal prosecutors have a clear vested interest in gang prevention and provide a vital link between knowledge and resources at the federal level, and action at the local level. The purpose of this article is to provide federal prosecutors with a firm knowledge of the foundations for gang prevention that are required to get results from the front end of local anti-gang initiatives. Successful gang prevention is based on the proper balance of (1) attractive alternatives to gangs, (2) effective support systems for young people, and (3) accountability of young people to their parents, schools, and communities. Discussed below are the principles of effective gang prevention, a framework for implementing them within a community-based anti-gang initiative, and information about resources to assist in these efforts.

Gang prevention is an effort to change the life trajectory of a young person who is otherwise likely to join a gang.

Why Youths Join Gangs

The image of the violent, anti-social gangster is part of the American landscape, often romanticized and glamorized by popular culture. Gang activity in the United States has been traced to the early 19th century when youth gangs emerged from some immigrant populations. Now, as then, gangs provide identity and social relationships for some young people who feel marginalized by the dominant social, economic and cultural environments in which they live. . . .

Historically, youth have been drawn to gangs because they increase a sense of self-worth and acceptance in individuals and hold out promises of higher status and personal protection. Gang affiliation can provide the status and peer acceptance important in adolescent development that is otherwise unavailable to at-risk youth.

National Youth Violence
Prevention Resource Center.
www.safeyouth.org.

Young people who join gangs are exercising a choice. The decision to join a gang is usually not made under extreme duress, though there are pressures placed on adolescents in this area. In fact, young people frequently see gangs as an attractive choice or a solution to their problems. From a practical perspective, gang prevention must address the needs and desires that underlie these choices in order to be effective. There are several sources of information on what young people want and what they need that have direct relevance to gang prevention. The first source of information on this topic comes from what we know about normal adolescent development.

Normal Adolescent Development

It is not a coincidence that the onset of adolescence overlaps with the average age for joining a gang (twelve to fourteen years old). The central developmental challenge of adolescence is described by psychologist Erik Erickson as "identity vs. role confusion." In short, all adolescents are trying to figure out who they are as they move toward adulthood. It is not uncommon for them to "try on" different identities during this time. This is a normal process that is harmless for most youth, but can also lead to risky and illegal behaviors.

The heightened importance of peer groups, and what psychologists call "egocentrism," are two other key developmental characteristics of adolescence. As children turn into adolescents, their focus of social attention and approval shifts from adults to their peers. During this time, adolescents become increasingly egocentric—meaning that they perceive the world as revolving around them—and they are deficient in the ability to accept other perspectives. Egocentrism has a number of consequences. For example, otherwise neutral events are more likely seen as personal slights, perceived injustices are often blown out of proportion, and the ability to empathize with others is underdeveloped. Taken together and applied in the context of a community with high levels of gang activity, normal adolescent development can result in very dangerous outcomes. Consider the common adolescent experience of being embarrassed or humiliated in front of a group of peers. This situation is difficult for any adolescent, but it can become deadly in the context of gang involvement. Gangs have access to illegal guns and norms that support violence as an appropriate method for resolving conflict. Many in local law enforcement are well aware of how frequently gang violence stems from seemingly minor "beefs" between adolescents.

Why Young People Join Gangs

Gang researchers Scott Decker and Barrik Van Winkle describe forces that "pull" and "push" young people into gangs.

If you ask current or former gang members, they are likely to describe the "pulls." That is, they will describe those attractive features of gang membership and the gang lifestyle that typically include respect, excitement, social opportunities, protection, and money. Respect in the context of gang membership translates more directly into intimidation or fear. Everyone wishes to be treated with respect, but gang membership offers young people a shortcut to earning respect. Excitement in the gang refers to risky behaviors, illegal activity, and generally upending the societal norms that define appropriate and inappropriate behavior, for example, parties where alcohol, drugs, and members of the opposite sex are readily available. The desire for protection among young people sometimes strikes a chord of compassion in adults. Some are tempted to ask, "Could it be that young people are really safer in gangs?" The answer is no. Despite myths to the contrary, gangs do not protect their members. Gang members are more likely to become victims because they embrace a lifestyle in which their own violence begets more violence. Finally, although some gangs and gang members make large sums of money through drug distribution or other criminal enterprises, many gangs lack the organizational sophistication to carry out these operations and, those that do, tend to concentrate most of the profits in the hands of a few people at the top. Thus, gang members often suggest motivations for joining gangs that seem like rational needs and desires. Gangs do not deliver on these promises, however, and the fun and excitement that are delivered lead to hazardous and destructive behaviors, that can be fatal or life altering.

Risk Factors

The forces that "push" young people into gangs have been verified by numerous . . . research studies that examine the conditions early in life that are related to an increased probability of gang membership in later years. Researchers have identified dozens of these conditions, called risk factors, that fall into five general categories or life domains. Researchers James "Buddy" Howell and Arlen Egley of the National Youth Gang Center (NYGC) recently summarized the five domains of risk factors for gang membership.

- Community or neighborhood risk factors—such as access to drugs, availability of illegal firearms, and the local crime rate.

- Family risk factors—such as sibling antisocial behavior, low parental control, and family poverty.

- School risk factors—such as low academic aspirations, low school attachment, and learning disabilities.

- Peer group risk factors—such as association with delinquent peers and/or aggressive peers.

- Individual risk factors—such as aggression or fighting, conduct disorders, and antisocial beliefs.

The more risk factors in the life of a young person, the greater the probability for joining a gang. A study of Seattle youth found that those with seven or more risk factors at age ten to twelve were thirteen times more likely to join a gang than those with no risk factors. This cumulative effect of risk factors is very important to gang prevention and intervention. No one risk factor rises clearly above the rest, and different configurations of risk factors are likely to be present in different communities and for different individuals. Thus, gang prevention and intervention efforts must be poised to identify those risk factors that are at play, determine which are most amenable to change, and target those with effective services at the community, family, or individual level.

Youth Have Many Needs

In summary, there are a variety of things that young people want and need that have direct relevance to gang prevention.

Adolescents need opportunities to explore their identity and the healthy paths to adulthood. They need to do this with their peers in a social setting that is safe. They want to have fun and excitement. They want to be respected. They want access to money. Indeed, many who work with and have studied at-risk youth find that they would be content simply to have improved access to meaningful employment. They have a wide variety of needs and personal challenges that fall into the five risk-factor domains related to their community, school, family, peers, and personal issues. The needs and desires of youth can point the way to alternatives that can compete with the features of gangs that attract them. These needs and desires also help us understand what is required for effective support systems. Superior gang prevention efforts blend effective support systems with attractive alternatives to gangs, and target these services to adolescents who are most at risk for gang involvement.

"An entire group of victims have been virtually ignored, diminishing the impact of potentially life-changing experiences among a group of youths who disproportionately come into contact with the juvenile and adult justice systems."

Victims of Violent Crimes Join Gangs

Terrance J. Taylor

In the following viewpoint, Terrance J. Taylor argues that there is an important relationship between victimization and gang membership though it has not been thoroughly studied. He notes that female gang members are more likely than nonmembers to have been the victims of violence in their homes and that seeking protection from this violence may be one of the important reasons girls join gangs. Terrance J. Taylor is an associate research professor in the Department of Criminology and Criminal Justice at the University of Missouri–St. Louis.

Terrance J. Taylor, "The Boulevard Ain't Safe for Your Kids. . .: Youth Gang Membership and Violent Victimization," *Journal of Contemporary Criminal Justice*, vol. 4, May 2008, pp. 125–133. Copyright © 2008 Sage Publications. Republished with permission of Sage Publications, conveyed through Copyright Clearance Center, Inc.

As you read, consider the following questions:

1. What did a study of eighth-grade students find about the relationship between gang membership and victimization?

2. What does the author say about victimization and youths who are associated with gangs but not gang members?

3. Do boys or girls experience more violent victimization?

Recent research has begun to examine the link between youth gang membership and violent victimization. Although studies of victimization in this area are sparse relative to those examining the link between gang membership and offending, the recent expansion to include victimization may be viewed as a promising development for a number of reasons. First, gang members' victimization has typically been hidden from public view or at least muted relative to their offending behaviors. Consequently, an entire group of victims have been virtually ignored, diminishing the impact of potentially life-changing experiences among a group of youths who disproportionately come into contact with the juvenile and adult justice systems. Second, youths who join gangs often report doing so for protection. Is this warranted? Do gangs reduce youths' victimization? Or do gangs actually enhance youths' victimization? Answers have real consequences for youths' future life chances.

The current essay looks at the research examining youth gang membership and violent victimization. . . . Three specific questions are examined. First, what does the extant [existing] research show regarding the linkage between gang membership and violent victimization? In other words, what do we know about the relationships between these phenomena? The essay is grouped into three sections, consistent with stages of gang membership: (a) victimization of gang members prior to their gang entry, (b) victimization during their time in the

Kids Are in Gangs or Are Victims

A survey highlighted in [Britain's] Channel 4's Dispatches ... shows that a shocking number of teenagers turn to violence—or are victims themselves.

Documentary makers quizzed 200 youths aged 11 to 18 on some of London and Glasgow's [Scotland] toughest estates [housing projects].

An amazing 84 of them admitted they were or had been caught up in gang life and committed serious violence against others.

And 112 said they had been victims of serious attacks—90 percent of which happened in the last 12 months. Teens told of being shot at, stabbed or threatened with knives and hit with blunt objects—but only 17 percent dared tell the police.

Sarah Jellema and Tom Carlin,
The People *(London), January 27, 2008.*

gang, and (c) victimization associated with gang exit and postgang membership. Second, what implications does this line of research have for practice (e.g., prevention and intervention programs)? We do have some knowledge on this topic, but what should we do? Specific policy recommendations are made in each section after the coverage of what we already know. Third, what questions remain unanswered? In other words, where do we go from here?

The Gang Membership–Violent Victimization Link

One early examination of the relationship between gang membership and victimization was conducted by [L.] Savitz, [L.]

Rosen, and [M.] Lalli (1980). Their surveys of approximately 1,000 Philadelphia boys found no statistically significant differences between gang and nongang youths in terms of fear of victimization or actual victimization experiences. Since that time, research has consistently demonstrated the increased risk of victimization—particularly violent victimization—of gang members relative to their nongang peers. Results from a 1995 cross-sectional study of 8th grade public school students in 11 U.S. cities highlight the relationships between gang membership and victimization. Gang members were found to be significantly more likely to be violently victimized during the past year, as well as to experience significantly more annual victimizations, than nongang youths for several types of violence. Substantively, the differences have been found to be quite large. For example, 70% of gang youths reported being the victim of general violence (assault, aggravated assault, and/or robbery), compared to 46% of nongang youths. Although most of the general violent victimization consisted of assaults (60% of gang members, 43% of nongang youths), differences in serious violent victimization (i.e., aggravated assault and/or robbery) were even more pronounced. During the past year, 44% of gang youths reported being victims of serious violence, with 38% of gang members reporting one or more aggravated assaults and 21% reporting one or more robberies during this time. Corresponding figures for nongang members were 12% for any type of serious violent victimization, 8% for aggravated assault, and 7% for robbery. Gang members who were victims also experienced significantly more violent victimization incidents (4.9 assaults, 3.8 aggravated, 4.1 robberies) than did nongang members who were victims (3.4 assaults, 2.7 aggravated assaults, 2.4 robberies) during the prior year.

Other Interesting Patterns

An interesting pattern to note involves the relationship between gang membership, sex, and violent victimization. Using data from the same cross-sectional study of 8th grade youths, [D.] Peterson, [T. J.] Taylor, and [F.-A.] Esbensen (2003) found that for each type of victimization (except robbery), gang males had the highest annual prevalence, followed by gang females (nongang males for robbery), then nongang males (nongang females for robbery), and then nongang females. Note that gang girls were more likely to report having been victimized than nongang boys for assault and aggravated assault. Gang member homicides, however, primarily remain the domain of males.

Finally, youths' "affiliation" with gangs appears to increase the risk of experiencing violent victimization, even if they are not gang members themselves. Limited information is available concerning the extent to which being heavily "embedded" in the gang (i.e., being a "core" member) insulates or enhances victimization, although [G. D.] Curry, [S. H.] Decker, and [A.] Egley's (2002) study of middle school youths found that simply being associated with gangs enhanced violent victimization. Although self-reported gang members were the most likely to report being threatened with a gun, shot at with a gun, and/or injured by a gunshot, the percentage of "gang affiliated" youths who reported experiencing these things were much higher than youths who reported no gang involvement whatsoever.

Victimization Prior to Gang Membership

Youths often report joining gangs for protection. For example, a 5-year longitudinal panel study of adolescents in seven U.S. cities found that 28% to 57% of self-identified gang youths indicated that they joined their gangs for protection. These percentages varied by the year of the survey/age of the respondents, with the lowest percentage reported among youths who joined gangs at the end of the study (when the average age was 16), and the highest reported during the third year (interestingly, the year most of the youths entered high school). From what are youths looking for protection?

Ethnographic studies on girl gang members provide some insight into this issue. Such studies have often found that girls join gangs to escape violently abusive home environments. For example, [J.] Miller's (2001) interviews with gang and non-gang girls in Columbus, Ohio, and St. Louis, Missouri, found that gang girls were significantly more likely to have witnessed and personally experienced physical and sexual violence in their homes. Many of the gang girls stated that they had begun associating with gang members in their neighborhoods— and eventually becoming gang members themselves—after spending more time away from home to escape the violence.

Boys and Victimization

From what are boys looking for protection? The answer to that question is more elusive. To date, this issue has received little attention. We are left with the following question: Are male gang members looking for protection from violent home environments, similar to those reported by girls? Or are boys looking to escape other types of victimization, such as from peers or community residents? Clearly, however, the answer is not that girls experience more violent victimization than boys, as official records (such as the Uniform Crime Reports), victimization surveys (such as the National Crime Victimization Survey), and surveys/interviews are quite consistent: Most forms of violent victimization (such as assault, aggravated assault, robbery, and homicide) are more common for young males than for young females. These sources also clearly illustrate that violent sexual offenses are more common for young females than for young males.

The answers to these questions are not only of interest to researchers—the recent increase in gender-specific programming information could benefit from it, as well. If boys and girls are joining gangs to escape similar forms of violence, more generalized prevention programs targeting the issue may be sufficient. However, if girls and boys are seeking protection from gangs for different forms of victimization, gender-specific prevention programming is vital. At this point, however, we do not know enough about sex differences in violent victimization prior to gang joining to definitively answer these questions.

| *"In today's society, many gang members compose and put their true-life experiences into lyrical form."*

The Rap Industry Exacerbates the Gang Problem

Donald Lyddane

In the following viewpoint, Donald Lyddane argues that gang members often compose rap music and this music provides insight into gang members' mentality. The author also believes that gang members launder money obtained from criminal activity through the sale of their music. Lyddane is an intelligence analyst assigned to the Safe Streets and Gang Unit at the Federal Bureau of Investigation.

As you read, consider the following questions:

1. How do many gang members produce and distribute their music, according to this viewpoint?

2. How, according to the author, is the entertainment industry responsible for the growth of gangs?

3. How, according to the author, do some gangs send coded messages to other gang members?

Donald Lyddane, "Understanding Gangs and Gang Mentality: Acquiring Evidence of the Gang Conspiracy," *The United States Attorneys' Bulletin,* vol. 54, May 2006, pp. 1–14. Reproduced by permission.

The following lyrical excerpts, taken from a CD entitled "Claiming My City," represent true-life proclamations of two prominent Washington, D.C. gang members. The lyrics, as recorded by them, verbalize their attitudes, motivations, and lifestyles.

> I got dope and coke and all and I'm selling it . . . I'm killin' motherf***ers for the hell of it. . . . I'm the little one, but my gun's a lot bigger . . . I can't wait to read about another dead n**ga in the g**damn obituary.
>
> *Claiming My City*
> *(Montana Records) (1992)*

One of those gang members, an executive producer for the record company, was reputed to be a significant drug dealer at a local public housing development. The other gang member was a primary enforcer for the gang that controlled the public housing development. His reputation as a killer was well-known to local law enforcement officers and other gang members. That gang member was later convicted of murder and is serving a life sentence.

In today's society, many gang members compose and put their true-life experiences into lyrical form. Many are able to record their lyrics at local recording studios, produce CDs, DVDs, and videos, and distribute these items to local music stores by using the proceeds of illegal criminal activities. Law enforcement officials must remain mindful of such money laundering schemes and the opportunities to obtain inculpatory [incriminating] evidence in gang-related investigations and cases. It is equally important to recognize that the lyrics demonstrate that the gangster lifestyle has become mainstream. It is now popular to be a "gangsta," the contemporary idiom for gangster.

A song like "Claiming My City" gives the reader a glimpse into the "gangsta" mentality. This article will explore gang mentality and the subsequent, anticipated behaviors of gang members that investigators and prosecutors may exploit to collect information and evidence in gang investigations.

Gangs and Gang Culture

A vast number of urban, suburban, and rural communities are plagued by street gangs who control drug markets in many of their neighborhoods, engage in violent crime, and create an atmosphere of fear within those communities. Crimes committed by gang members are not restricted to gang-sanctioned offenses. The lifestyle of drug trafficking, violence, and greed has created individuals whose value system is counter to that of society at large. Gang members will engage in criminal activities with little regard for the lives or safety of others. This lifestyle has contributed to increased drug trafficking, violent crime, and other criminal activity, which negatively impacts the quality of life in many communities. Neighborhood-based gangs often control all, or at least a portion of, the retail drug distribution in those areas. Their "retail labor force," those who sell drugs hand-to-hand at the street level, often are the neighborhood teenagers who join gangs for several reasons.

For many teens, the primary motive to become a gang member is money. However, gang membership and lifestyle go beyond economic motivation. Identity and recognition are powerful motivational factors to many teenagers. Many gang trends such as "colors," hand signs, graffiti, "gang writings," and tattoos, among other things are directly related to the desire of the gang member to be identified with, and recognized as, a member of a particular gang. To many, a gang constitutes a type of extended family. Gang identification symbols are merely visible signs of a powerful group identity and unity, which are built on the simplest of bases—loyalty to fellow members and to gang territory.

The news media and entertainment industry have sensationalized gang crimes and the gang lifestyle to the point that it has become part of mainstream America. This has contrib-

Gang Rap

Hip hop identity is now a world-wide phenomena, the cutting edge of global youth culture. The "gangsta" identity both represents the drama of the steets, but also the "merchandizing of the rhymes of violence" by profit hungry media companies. As [rapper] KRS-1 and others tell it, the media companies promote the most outrageous stereotypes of "violent, vicious" Black youth while ignoring the rappers who represent the positive and political side of ghetto life.

GangResearch.net. *www.uic.edu.*

uted to the emergence, migration, and growth of a popular "gangsta" subculture. Music, magazines, movies, and the Internet serve as training vehicles on how to be a "gangsta." Increasingly, young teens are at great risk of being seduced by, and recruited into, this way of life. The promises of respect, money, expensive clothes, cars, and other inducements, put youths from all backgrounds, neighborhoods, and income levels at risk.

The Spread of Gang Culture

This subculture has spread beyond the borders of the United States. For example, several years ago authorities in Cape Town, South Africa, who were struggling with a gang problem, invited gang expert, Sergeant Wes McBride of the Los Angeles County Sheriff's Department (now retired) to visit their city and examine the problem. After carefully evaluating the situation, which included interviews with Cape Town gang members, Sergeant McBride concluded, "they are just like our gangs." He reported that the gangs were influenced by American music and films and emulated the American gang subculture. One gang even called itself the "Americans."

It is no accident that gang styles of music, language, and clothing have made a considerable impact on popular youth culture. As previously mentioned, gangs represent a powerful group identity, and the members are surrounded with the appealing aura of outlaw danger. The wearisome and cruel reality of gang life rarely matches the fantasy, yet the power of the myth remains undiminished.

The vast majority of gangs in the United States are community or neighborhood-based and adversely impact small geographical areas. Local gangs can be just as violent and dangerous, if not more so, than nationally recognized gangs. Some gangs, however, rapidly grow in size and sophistication, becoming multijurisdictional, even international in nature, and can adversely impact countless communities across this and other nations. Some prominent outlaw motorcycle gangs have evolved into international organized crime enterprises. Many prison gangs, such as the California Mexican Mafia, continue to evolve into sophisticated criminal enterprises, which control the criminal activities of street gangs. Nationally recognized gangs, such as the Bloods, Crips, Mara Salvatrucha 13, 18th Street, Gangster Disciples, Almighty Latin Kings and Queens Nation, and Vice Lords Nation continue to demonstrate a propensity for violence and the ability to migrate and establish criminal networks in multiple communities. . . .

Lyrics and Productions

Many gang members compose hip-hop lyrics that reflect true-life experiences. Search warrants of homes and jail cells often net such writings. The contents of these writings frequently reflect the author's gang mentality and, in some cases, result in solid investigative leads. Occasionally, the writings can be used as evidence. Many gang members frequent clubs where they can perform their songs, and a number of clubs record the performances for later sale. Composing lyrics and committing them to print is not limited to any particular gang. . . .

Some gang members will produce and distribute audio and video recordings for sale in local music stores. This media and the associated packaging may also contain information of investigative value in a gang case. In addition, the gang investigator should be aware that gangs may launder money through the sale of these items.

Home Videos

Individuals and families capture special moments and document their lives through photographs and home videos. Gang members do the same. Investigators should take the time to locate and review every photograph, video, and home DVD and CD when executing search warrants. Gang members sometimes record their own criminal offenses and various gang events. This author participated in a case in which a home video, recovered as part of a gang investigation, revealed a gang member displaying guns, drugs, and cash in front of his young children, while "gangsta" rap recordings played in the background. That song's lyrics, "I got money and the power, money and the power," could be heard in the background as the gang member flashed cash toward the video camera and, with the help of his four-year-old son, bagged what appeared to be a large amount of crack cocaine.

Entertainment

Know where the local gang members seek entertainment. Ask where, and in which clubs, do they hangout? Are there cable televison shows that feature local gangs and/or local gang members who are also budding entertainers? Are there radio stations that host "shout-out" hours where gang members can call in and "shout-out" their names and the names of their gangs? If so, do gang members use that air-time to pass messages? An FBI [Federal Bureau of Investigation] case in El

Paso, Texas, revealed that incarcerated gang members called into such radio shows to deliver coded messages in their "shout-outs." In Washington, D.C., a cable television station aired a show that featured local hip-hop artists and gang members, which was filmed in their gang neighborhoods. Gang violence is prevalent in night clubs, bars, and similar gang hangouts and such violence can precipitate more intense confrontations in the community. It is recommended that investigators monitor police reporting of complaints, recovered firearms, and arrests at and around the specific establishments frequented by gang members.

> *"Gangsta rap is the power of negativity to keep on living in the awareness of ghetto conditions that are unlikely to be improved by government, business, or liberal whites."*

The Relationship Between Rap and Gangs Has Been Misunderstood

John M. Hagedorn

In the following viewpoint, John M. Hagedorn explains that hip hop and rap music had their origins as a force to liberate urban youth from the hardships of street life in the ghettos of cities such as New York. He argues that hip hop is not about instigating violent behavior but about youth searching for their identity in bleak circumstances and sharing with the world the reality of life in the ghettos. John M. Hagedorn is an associate professor in the Department of Criminal Justice at the University of Illinois at Chicago.

As you read, consider the following questions:

1. How does the author explain the relationship between hip hop and gangsta rap?

John M. Hagedorn, *A World of Gangs: Armed Young Men and Gangsta Culture.* Minneapolis: University of Minnesota Press, 2008, pp. 93–98. Copyright © 2008 by the Regents of the University of Minnesota. All rights reserved. Reproduced by permission.

2. What did Afrika Bambaataa think hip hop could do for street youth, according to the author?

3. Why, according to the author, is gangsta rap so popular?

Hip-hop today is torn by a searing "culture war" between two different resistance identities: a defiant but life-affirming "black Atlantic hip-hop" and the consumer-oriented "corporate hip-hop" that now controls gangsta rap. This chapter [of *A World of Gangs*] seeks to understand the contradictions within hip-hop and how they shape, and are shaped by, the multiple conflicting identities of gang members.

Hip-Hop and Culture

Rather than locate a "gang subculture" in different kinds of neighborhood "opportunity structures," or as an epiphenomenon of larger, more "fundamental" structural forces, this chapter argues that hip-hop is a central way for gang members and other young people (and some not so young) to make meaning out of their lives. . . . I see culture as reflecting and reproducing structural conditions, but also rising above them as a powerful, independent force in its own right. In other words, culture is responsive, but also transformative. It is reproductive, but also productive.

In the face of desperate ghetto conditions and the permanence of racism, some claim that "hip hop has become the primary vehicle for transmitting culture and values to this generation, relegating black families, community centers, churches, and schools to the back burner." While this may be an overstatement, in many ways the key to understanding gangs is to "get" their music: where it came from, what it represents, why they like it, and what potential it can tap.

A Brief History of Gangs and Hip-Hop

Hip-hop is a worldwide street culture and consists of four elements: MCing (or rapping), DJing (spinning and scratching records), breakdancing, and graffiti art. Some say that "Rappers Delight," a 1979 song by the Sugar Hill Gang, is the source of the term *hip-hop*: the song begins with the lyrics "da hip da hop, da hippity da hip hip hop and you don't stop." Others say [early rap artist] Lovebug Starski coined the term much earlier. Gangsta rap is a subgenre of hip-hop, and while it is a hyperbolic representation of street culture, it is also a big moneymaker for media conglomerates like Time Warner.

Hip-hop had its immediate origins in the music, dance, and art of African American and Latino youth in the South Bronx in the early 1970s. As a musical form, it is notable that it came from the streets, not the studios. Like the "devil's music" of the blues, it is not based in middle-class experience but in an expression of the dispossessed's misery and defiance of racism and poverty. The South Bronx of the seventies was the perfect environment for the rise of hip-hop. Some 170,000 black and Latino peoples had been dislocated because of [urban planner] Robert Moses's Cross-Bronx Expressway and other "urban development" projects. Communities were shattered and left leaderless. Arson cleared out whole areas, making the South Bronx look like it had been bombed. The area became the symbol of the desolation and poverty of blacks and Puerto Ricans in the United States.

In Chicago and Los Angeles [LA], similar situations of turmoil produced powerful gangs that became entrenched in their communities. New York City too had well-known gangs, and many more of them at the time than Chicago or Los Angeles. If ever an opportunity existed that would allow gangs to persist and become major forces in their communities, it would have been the South Bronx in the 1970s. Yet, unlike Chicago and LA, older gangs in the Bronx faded, with the inevitable new, younger ones taking their place. Why?

New York City under [mayor] John Lindsay did not declare war on gangs, as did [mayor] Richard J. Daley in Chicago and [mayor] Samuel Yorty in LA, but attempted to reach out to the ghettos. The importance of Lindsay's modest social opportunities policy may not have been what it did but what it did *not* do—try to suppress gangs by large-scale incarceration. Rather than prison aiding the institutionalization of gangs and assisting them to become the center of youthful rebellion, the streets hosted a new musical form.

The Role of Afrika Bambaataa

The key figure is not Lindsay, however, but Afrika Bambaataa, the "godfather of hip-hop." As one of the first MCs, his vision for hip-hop has remained one pole of an intense cultural struggle among youth today. Bambaataa, whose given name is Kevin Donovan, was a "warlord" in the Bronx River Project division of the Black Spades, one of that area's largest, most-feared street gangs. Unlike Bobby Gore, a Chicago singer (the Clevertones) and leader of the [gang] Vice Lords, Bambaataa was not targeted for arrest and prison. Instead he left the gang and turned his talents to use music to lure kids from the violent life of the streets.

Bambaataa was enthralled with all types of musical styles and seized on and popularized the rapping of street youth, the scratching of records, and roles of DJ and MC at street parties. His music joined with other innovators, like Kool Herc, a transplanted Jamaican who introduced the Trenchtown system of setting up large speakers on street corners, turning South Bronx neighborhoods into raucous block parties.

Bambaataa early on saw that music and the not-yet-named hip-hop had the potential to pull kids from the self-hatred and destructive behavior that is an all-too-common response to poverty and racism. "At some point he started to believe," [sociologist] S. Craig Watkins says in his incisive *Hip Hop Matters*, "that the energy, loyalty, and passion that defined gang life could be guided toward more socially productive activities." Bambaataa went on to found a performing group

The Inaccurate Image of Gangs in Rap

[Bruce George]: There's a difference between "industry" and "in the streets." Those so-called rap artists who are seen in rap videos portraying a lifestyle of "thugdom" and "gangdom" seldom have had any experience with what they are projecting. They are basically satisfying the wishes of the powers that be that make money off of the death of black and brown folk. That's why when a famous rapper/emcee dies, the record company makes more revenue than when that rapper/emcee was alive and kicking, [as seen with] Tupac Shakur and Biggie Smalls.

Those in rap videos who falsely posture as gang members are responsible for the proliferation and bastardization of gang culture. This in turn has led to there being copycat gangs across the country that try to fit their frame of reference into the contours of L.A. gangs like the Crips/Bloods. In turn, you have a crop of gangs popping up that have no structure, unity, loyalty and knowledge of the particular set they are claiming. A lot of them are not studying or applying their lessons properly. For instance, the word "Blood" is an acronym for "Brotherly Love Overrides Oppressive Destruction," and the word "Crip" stands for "Community Revolution in Progress."

Brian Sims interviewing Bruce George,
co-founder of Def Poetry Jam, October 13, 2007.
HipHopDX.com.

called The Organization, then later formed the Zulu Nation, a remarkable collective of New York artists that included Queen Latifah and LL Cool J.

Hip-Hop and Identity

Hip-hop emerged, [author and professor] Tricia Rose eloquently points out,

> from the deindustrialization meltdown where social alienation, prophetic imagination, and yearning intersect. Hip hop is a cultural form that attempts to negotiate the experiences of marginalization, brutally truncated opportunity, and oppression within the cultural imperatives of African-American and Caribbean history, identity, and community.

Hip-hop would have many facets, but was essentially created as an oppositional form of identity, reflecting Bronx youth's collective struggle for self-recognition and meaning in bleak surroundings. "Alternative local identities were forged in fashion and language, street names, and most important, in establishing neighborhood crews or posses."

In other words, rather than the identity of gang member, what took the South Bronx by storm was a racialized, oppositional identity based in culture. Watkins explains that Afrika Bambaataa professed, "Hip hop's real power and true significance resides in its capacity to empower young people to change their lives." [Philosopher] Cornel West sums up the essence of hip-hop culture:

> The basic aims of hip-hop music are threefold—to provide playful entertainment and serious art for the rituals of young people, to forge new ways of escaping social misery, and to explore novel responses for meaning and feeling in a market-driven world.

Other Cultural Influences on Hip-Hop

To be sure, hip-hop did not spring like a rapping Minerva from the head of Afrika Bambaataa. While some want to define hip-hop as "authentic" black culture, in reality hip-hop is a marvelous hybrid, a merger of earlier blues, the West African griot, or call and response and emphasis on drumming, the Afro-Brazilian martial arts dance capoeira, and the Jamaican toasting tradition, as well as the African American celebration of male outlaws like "Stagger Lee." Puerto Rican and other Latino influences were present in New York in the early years, and Mexican influences helped shape West Coast rap. West African and Jamaican music, among others, make hiphop essentially a "black Atlantic" culture, to extend an idea from [sociologist] Paul Gilroy's seminal work.

Borrowing heavily from [early twentieth-century civil rights activist and sociologist] W. E. B. DuBois's concept of "double consciousness," Gilroy points out that "black culture"—like hip-hop—derives from many African, Caribbean, and European influences. The diversity of this culture is, in fact, its strength, speaking in many different voices and with many different messages. . . . The struggle over these contradictory tendencies and various identities, I argue, is of central importance for the future of our youth.

The Two Faces of Gangsta Rap

Gangsta rap has always been a powerful voice as one kind of hardcore rap. Gangsta rap has been popular, in essence, because it expresses the rage of the gang member in the ghetto and his defiance of the white man's system, particularly the police. This black rage has always found a cultural outlet, in music with the blues, and in the angry, passionate writings of [novelists] Richard Wright, James Baldwin, Toni Morrison, and many others. For example, Eldridge Cleaver, the former convict and Black Panther, shocked many with *Soul on Ice* by writing that the rape of white women was "an insurrectionary act . . . defying and trampling on the white man's law."

What is often missed in the numerous denunciations of Cleaver's quite real ideas of male supremacy is his self-reflection over this rage on the book's very next page. There Cleaver says that he could not "approve the act of rape," that his actions as a rapist cost him his "self-respect." The man,

Cleaver, vowed to give his rage a cultural solution: "That is why I started to write. To save myself." This became Cleaver's way of reacting to nihilism [a philosophy that believes life is meaningless]. Similarly, the "rage" that comes from recognition of "the permanence of racism" sets both the emotional and creative conditions for the emergence of the cultural response of gangsta rap.

The popularity of gangsta rap comes from its ironic and defiant nature, its hardcore beats, and its very negativity in a world that appears unchangeable. At times, [rapper] Ice Cube says, "there is no message, just reality." [Rapper] Ice-T adds: "This music isn't supposed to be positive. It's supposed to be negative, because the streets are negative." Ice Cube argues that gangsta rap is hated because it is telling the truth about the ghetto, not sugarcoating racism and poverty. "We tell kids the truth. . . . The world is an ugly place."

In Defense of Gangsta Rap

Pious condemnations of "gangsta rap" by notables like [former senator] Bob Dole or [former president] Bill Clinton ring hollow when these same politicians shamelessly accept millions in campaign contributions from the movie stars of Hollywood, America's first and foremost evil empire of sex and violence. Many denunciations of the influence of rap on young people are humorless, missing its irony and how rappers poke fun at white America. How else are we to understand [rapper] Tupac Shakur's hilarious taunt that listening to him is like watching "OJ All-Day. Picture me 'Rollin!'"? Or enjoy any video from the aptly named "Ludacris."

[Historian] Robin D. G. Kelley tries to counter the moral majority tide by pointing to rap's cultural nature: "Lest we get too sociological here, we must bear in mind that hip hop, irrespective of its particular flavor, is music."

The power of gangsta rap to thrill black youth is why important, street-smart black religious figures like Louis Farrakhan have come to its defense and worked directly with rappers to organize gang truces and stop the violence. Gangsta rap is the power of negativity to keep on living in the awareness of ghetto conditions that are unlikely to be improved by government, business, or liberal whites. It is a "form of 'testimony' for the underclass" and its gangs. Like the blues, its style and message can "stare painful truths in the face and persevere without cynicism or pessimism."

The Music Industry

But that said, gangsta rap is more than words of rebellion. In the early nineties, rap's east coast and west coast represented ganglike enemies and a feud that would cost hip-hop some its most talented stars, such as Tupac and the Notorious B.I.G. Those wars were real and lethal, but also a grim reflection of the music industry's amoral capacity to exploit even murder for profit.

Keith Clinkscales, in 1997 the CEO of *Vibe*, a prominent hip-hop magazine, said that the "marketing of evil" is a "double-edged sword." "Murder," Clinkscales argued, apparently without irony, "is not good for business." While Clinkscales personally cannot "condone some of the nihilism and misogynistic [woman-hating] elements," hip-hop artists, he says, "should have the opportunity to have their work judged by the market." The sound you hear is not "hip, hippity, hop" but "ka-ching."

"The NF isn't a street gang that's gone to prison. It's a prison gang that's hit the streets."

Gangs Are Proliferating in Prisons

Michael Montgomery

In the following viewpoint, Michael Montgomery explains that gangs such as the Latino gang Nuestra Familia (NF) started in the very prisons which were meant stifle them. According to Montgomery, the leaders of NF run complex criminal networks from inside California's Pelican Bay State Prison, and gang members outside the prison look forward to going to prison so that they can meet and learn from other gang members. Michael Montgomery is a correspondent and writer for Minnesota Public Radio.

As you read, consider the following questions:

1. What does the author say was Epitacio Cortina's job for the Nuestra Familia (NF) gang?

2. How do the NF leaders control street gangs from inside the prison, according to the author?

Michael Montgomery, "Locked Down: Gangs in the Supermax," *American RadioWorks*, 2008. Reproduced by permission.

3. How does gang member Willie Stokes describe his first
days in prison?

Twenty years ago, a new kind of prison was taking America
by storm. The supermax prison was designed to incapacitate dangerous criminals by locking them down in stark isolation, sometimes for years on end.

So have the supermaxes lived up to their promise of stopping violent criminals?

Pelican Bay State Prison in California is one of America's
biggest supermaxes, but it is not just a supermax. It's also
headquarters to some of America's biggest and most violent
prison gangs. Experts say these gangs control crime far outside prison walls. . . .

Cap's Saloon is a bar and card room in downtown Salinas,
California. On a warm evening in May, 2001, Armando Frias
Jr. was there playing pool. Frias was 19 years old and an aspir-
ing member of a gang that controlled drug sales in the area.
At Cap's he spotted a man who was in trouble with the gang
for selling drugs without sharing his profits. Frias called his
street bosses on his cell phone. They met him in the parking
lot. They gave him a gun, and he went back inside.

"When I walked in there," says Frias, "I went to the juke-
box, came up behind him, and shot him. I thought I hit him
in the back of the head and I found out I hit him in the back
of the neck."

The victim died at the scene. Armando Frias Jr. was arrested and imprisoned. But the leaders of the group behind
the killing were already in prison. Frias was acting on behalf
of a powerful Latino prison gang. The group is called "Our
Family"—in Spanish, Nuestra Familia, or NF.

"All over Northern California," Frias explains, "you've got
these regiments that are being run by the NF, and all these
regular street gang members out there selling drugs, they're

paying a certain percentage to the NF. They call it paying rent or taxes. That's just the way the NF runs, that's the way they run the streets."

Flourishing Prison Gangs

The NF isn't a street gang that's gone to prison. It's a prison gang that's hit the streets. The NF and other prison gangs have flourished in a place designed to shut them down.

At Pelican Bay State Prison, behind a maze of concrete walls, high voltage security fences and steel doors, lies a prison within a prison. It's commonly known as a supermax. The state of California calls this place the Security Housing Unit or SHU.

Most of the inmates in the SHU are gang members. Their cells are windowless and nearly bare. The men are locked inside for 22 and a half hours a day, usually alone. They are held in virtual isolation to try to keep them from working together, but even the SHU can't stop some leaders from running their gangs.

Joseph McGrath was warden at Pelican Bay until 2004.

"The head leaders of the Nuestra Familia, the Mexican Mafia, the Aryan Brotherhood, you name the prison gang, they're in prison," says McGrath. "And they control the activities of the gang both within the prison system and in our communities in California and now unfortunately, have even spread to other states."

Prison gangs that started in California are now in more than 20 states. Recent surveys report more than 300,000 gang members in America's jails and prisons. For convicts like Epitacio Cortina, the prison gang offered a strange kind of career: as teacher, fighter, arch criminal.

"I lived, I breathed, I ate, I slept, I thought the gang," says Cortina.

He is a heavy set, 31-year-old Latino serving 15 years to life for murder. His body is covered with NF tattoos, a black eagle with arched wings on his wrist, the number 14 etched just above his left eye. Cortina spent eight years in the Pelican Bay SHU as a loyal captain in the Nuestra Familia.

Creating a Criminal Network

"When I became a member of the NF," says Cortina, "I was put in charge of a regiment out on the streets, meaning I was to help oversee that regiment making sure that the members we had out there were generating revenue for the organization in prison."

Cortina says he trained other inmates prior to their parole. Once out of prison, these men ran the gang's criminal network, including street gangs.

"We'd educate them on vocabulary, how to speak properly, how to dress properly, blend in with society so that way you can do your criminal activity on the under. We also educated them on how to do bank robberies, how to do armored car robberies, how to do home invasions."

Cortina says the parolees faced brutal retaliation if they didn't follow the gang's orders. Cortina himself is now in danger because he recently left the gang.

NF generals at the Pelican Bay SHU controlled dozens of street regiments like Cortina's. Twenty-five percent of profits, mainly from drug dealing, was deposited in NF bank accounts. To do all this, the gang used ingenious methods.

Sending Messages from Prison

"We've got several examples of what we call micro-writing," says officer David Barneburg, as he shows off a pile of recently intercepted messages.

The NF passes messages in legal mail and in scraps of paper filled with tiny, almost microscopic script.

"This is what we refer to as a BNL, a bad news list," says Barneburg. "This one I've got is actually 14 pages long and contains about 1500 names of northern Hispanics, their CDC

[California Department of Corrections] number, any marks or tattoos they have that we can identify them by. Whenever somebody arrives to a yard, this list will be referenced. If their name is on the list, they'll be targeted for assault. And this is only a partial list."

"That list was recovered from a northern Hispanic in the B facility of the prison," Barneburg continues. "It was recovered by the staff and had been secreted in the inmate's rectum."

Gang members don't just hide messages in body cavities. They also write them in exotic languages. This method is so pervasive, Pelican Bay actually banned anything written in Swahili, Celtic, Runic and Nahuatl, an Aztec language used by the Nuestra Familia.

"Every time we tighten the screws so to speak, they're going to find a way around it," says [Lieutenant] Robert Marquez, Pelican Bay's chief gang investigator. He says even though guards read inmates' mail and monitor their phone calls, gang leaders still get their orders out onto the streets. "If they know a certain gang member's paroling they'll give him all kinds of messages, phone numbers, contacts, hit lists. So the guy leaves here with a cache of information [of] people who are supposed to be murdered, people who are supposed to be extorted."

The Problem in Salinas

Out of prison flows crime. No place has been hit harder than Salinas, the farming town in central California that once inspired John Steinbeck.

In an east Salinas neighborhood with rows of tidy houses, three men in their late teens stand in an open garage. They are members of a street gang with close links to the Nuestra Familia. One man, who calls himself Juan, is sealing a drug deal on his cell phone.

Governor Schwarzenegger Calls for a Coordinated Anti-Gang Effort

"A growing number of Californians are living a nightmare trapped inside their homes, afraid to come out unless they absolutely have to. That's because in many of our cities, whole neighborhoods are terrorized and intimidated by street gangs. Kids are scared to go to school and parents are terrified for their safety," said Governor Schwarzenegger. . . .

For the past several months the Governor has met with mayors, law enforcement, faith-based and community organizations, local officials and legislators to discuss how communities across the state are fighting gangs and what resources they need to strengthen their success. At every meeting the Governor heard about the same problems: lack of coordination between state and local agencies and programs, lack of funding, and lack of a comprehensive approach to anti-gang efforts. "Everywhere I went, local law enforcement would say the problem is just being pushed from one city to the next. They say gang leaders come out of state prisons and go right back to terrorizing their communities—law enforcement finds out they have gang leaders back in their communities when gang-related violence spikes. Prosecutors say they need more tools to protect witnesses. Community leaders say they can get kids out of gangs but they need help with job training and education. The State spends hundreds and hundreds of millions of dollars on education, job training and substance abuse treatment every year—with no focused coordination on gang activities. . . ."

California Department of Corrections and Rehabilitation, 2007.

The men wear short hair, red baseball caps, and football jerseys. With pride, they show off torsos etched with gang tattoos and scars from bullet wounds.

"I believe in being a homeboy," says Juan. "I just believe I will die for my cause, for my struggle."

Juan says the struggle is about defending northern California Latinos, called "norteños," from the enemy, Latinos with roots in southern California, known as "sureños." But it's really a struggle for drug turf that began behind bars with two long-feuding prison gangs: the NF, which spawned the norteños, and the Mexican Mafia, an even bigger prison gang that rallies the sureños.

The proxy war between northern and southern California Latinos has claimed hundreds of lives. It burns in places like Salinas where poverty and unemployment are severe.

Now, some people are getting fed up with the violence. Demonstrators in Salinas recently gathered to mourn the city's 250th gang related killing since the early 1990s. They beat drums, chanted and watch Aztec-style dancing.

Not all the victims are gang members. Elsa Sandoval came here to remember her 27-year-old son Joey. He was killed two years ago in what appeared to be a random shooting. His murder, like many in Salinas, remains unsolved.

"We won't stop," says Sandoval, "until we find these son-of-a-bitches that killed our sons. We'll find them."

The Changing Character of the NF

NF old timers say this kind of street violence is not what the group was founded for. Like many prison gangs, the NF started as a prisoner defense group in the late 1960s. The NF established a constitution and an educational curriculum. But the NF moved into the drug trade and grew more violent.

The NF expanded into youth jails and onto the streets. Leaders imposed military-style discipline and a lifetime commitment often sealed in the killing of a rival.

By the late 1990s, law enforcement started to see the true scale of the NF. George Collord, a police detective in Santa Rosa, was investigating unsolved gang murders when an informant linked the crimes to Pelican Bay. His investigation later triggered a major FBI [Federal Bureau of Investigation] task force. Collord was stunned to discover a sophisticated gang network throughout northern California—all controlled by NF leaders in Pelican Bay's Security Housing Unit.

"Generally people in this country think that when people go to prison, that they're losers," says Collord. "These guys were not losers."

The Spread of Gang Culture

Collord started calling the NF leaders "puppet masters." He discovered the gang even produced low-budget films and rap CDs with chilling lyrics. One such song, "Target Practice," has a chorus of females repeating "Pinta bound, pinta bound," which means headed for prison. This song's message is that prison is inevitable—even desirable.

Collord says the CDs flew off the shelves and triggered more violence.

"There's always been gangster rap around," says Collord, "but this was a little more direct in its approach. It had a selected audience which were the young northern Hispanics that the NF really wanted to recruit and tell them that, 'You're not alone. You've got a huge army, a huge movement that is with you.'"

Aspiring Gang Members

That message inspired young street gang members like Willie Stokes. That's why he arrived to Pelican Bay filled with the anticipation of a college freshman.

"When I first went to Pelican Bay," says Stokes, "you're like so fascinated by, 'Oh here's all these guys you've always heard about, all these guys who run everything.' You're just fascinated with it all. And you hear the way they talk, Aztec language, just all this knowledge and philosophy from reading all this stuff. You just, you know, 'Oh I want to be like that, I want to be smart and educated like he sounds.'"

"I've sat in rooms with young kids, who say they can't wait to go to prison," says George Collord. "Because their uncles have gone, their cousins have gone, the people they respect most in this world have gone to prison. And you scratch your head, and you go, 'Wait a second, you want to give up your freedom out here?' I've even said, 'You want to give up girls for a while? Come on, you're a teenager!' 'Yes,' the answer's 'yes.'"

But before a young gang member gets to prison, he's expected to put in work on the streets. That might mean assaulting a rival, or murder. And that brings the story back to Armando Frias Jr.

On that warm May evening at Cap's Saloon, Frias was fresh out of juvenile lockup where he'd enlisted with a group run by the NF. Frias says some members had doubts about his loyalty because of relatives who'd dropped out of the gang.

"So I used to go out of my way to show that there was no reason for them to have doubts about me," says Frias. "And I don't like nobody to question me. And the way I did was by showing them through my actions."

At Cap's Saloon, a video surveillance camera recorded Frias proving his loyalty by shooting a man named Raymond Sanchez. Frias is now serving 25 years to life for the murder.

Frias was one of dozens of people prosecuted as part of the FBI-led crackdown on the Nuestra Familia. They include five NF leaders indicted while serving life terms at Pelican Bay Prison. Detective George Collord says the operation was a success and that the NF's leadership is disrupted, for now.

"But the years and years of training and the philosophies that have gone down," says Collord, "from the thousands that are below them, leaders will emerge. As long as you've got the recruitment pool out there, you're going to survive and new leaders will emerge."

There is an epilogue to this story. The five Nuestra Familia leaders prosecuted in federal court are apparently still in business. Intercepted communications revealed the NF leaders were issuing orders, even as they awaited probable life sentences from a federal judge. The men will serve their time far away from California, but now investigators believe the NF is plotting to expand to federal prison.

> "It has often been said that prison is a microcosm of the outside world, and as such, within the New Jersey Department of Corrections (NJDOC), the gang issue has been actively addressed since the late 1980s."

Prison Managers Are Effectively Fighting the Proliferation of Gangs in Prisons

Ron Holvey

In the following viewpoint, Ron Holvey describes how the New Jersey Department of Corrections is combating gang activity and proliferation in New Jersey's prisons and in the community. He explains that gang members are identified at prisoner intake, isolated from other prisoners, and required to participate in an anti-violence course. Furthermore, he describes how a program has been set up to keep track of inmate gang members after they are released back into the community. Holvey works for the New Jersey Department of Corrections and is vice president of the East Coast Gang Investigators Association.

Ron Holvey, "Fighting Gangs in our Prisons and Neighborhoods," *New Jersey Municipalities Magazine*, September 2005. Reproduced by permission.

As you read, consider the following questions:

1. Why, according to the author, are prisoners so carefully photographed at intake?
2. What evidence does the author give that the Security Threat Group Management Unit program is successful?
3. What is the purpose of the Combined Law Enforcement Intelligence Committee, according to the author?

The news from the New Jersey State Police was nothing less than shocking—there are nearly 17,000 gang members statewide. These sobering statistics, released on June 30, 2005, confirm what law enforcement already suspected—the plague that is gangs is no longer relegated solely to the barrios [neighborhoods] of East Los Angeles, or the bowels of Rikers Island [New York City prison]. Indeed, from the picturesque mountains of Sussex County, to the beaches of Atlantic City, and everywhere in between, gangs are proliferating. And while urban centers continue to be the principal home turf for street gangs, the suburbs are reporting an increased gang presence and the inevitable crime and victimization that follow.

Gangs have been in existence for decades, but the veritable explosion in the "gangster" mentality is a true child of the 21st century. Pop culture, to include music and dress, coupled with those electronic marvels, computers, iPods and cell phones, which serve as a conduit to youngsters everywhere, has served to spread the word that gang membership is not only acceptable, but desirable.

Controlling Gangs in Prison

It has often been said that prison is a microcosm of the outside world, and as such, within the New Jersey Department of Corrections (NJDOC), the gang issue has been actively addressed since the late 1980s. As gang members are apprehended and convicted for criminal misconduct in the community, they are rightfully placed behind prison and jail walls.

This circumstance does not in and of itself mean that upon their incarceration the offender disavows his/her gang affiliation or gang-related proclivities. Thus, as more and more gang members are brought to justice, their numbers in our correctional system grow, increasing security demands in an already highly challenged environment.

Thus, the Intelligence Section of the department's Special Investigations Division has made gang management within the prisons a priority.

The Three-Part Gang Management Program

This process begins at the prison intake, with each inmate interviewed and photographed, as tattoos and possession of gang-related paraphernalia often speak volumes about gang affiliation, even if the inmate does not. Identified gang members are advised that any future gang activity will not be tolerated and that noncompliance will have serious consequences.

When it became apparent that such a large number of inmates were identified definitively as gang members, the NJ-DOC designed a special unit to house the gang leaders apart from the general population. To that end, The Security Threat Group Management Unit (STGMU), located at Northern State Prison in Newark, was devised to isolate problematic gang affiliated inmates or those identified as gang leaders from the general prison population. The STGMU provides a structured and controlled environment where inmate behavior is closely monitored by a multidiscipline team of departmental staff.

To successfully complete the three-phase program, inmates are required to participate in programs that deal with such areas as alternatives to violent behavior, cognitive development and non-violent living. The goal is to enlighten the inmates and teach them the skills necessary to interact appropriately without the perceived need of gang membership. This program is also intended to force inmates to deal with the consequences of their actions. Prior to moving through the program, inmates are required to sign an "Acknowledgment of Expectations" for each phase that clearly outlines their responsibilities for successful program completion and ultimately requires offenders to renounce their Security Threat Group affiliation prior to completion. The results of the STGMU program were immediate—the department has seen a system-wide drop of 42 percent in staff assaults and an 84 percent decrease in organized violent behavior among our inmates.

Furthermore, recent data shows that gang members who have completed the Security Threat Group Management Unit (STGMU) program recidivate [return to criminal behavior] at less than half the rate of the national average for prisoners who are released to the community. These statistics underscore the effectiveness of this approach. The fact that Maryland and North Carolina, among others, are modeling their gang units after the NJDOC's STGMU unit indicates that the department is not alone in reaching that assessment.

Managing Gangs in the Community

Currently, seven gangs have been classified as Security Threat Groups by the NJDOC: the Almighty Latin King and Queen Nation, Bloods, Crips, East Coast Aryan Brotherhood, Five Percent Nation, Neta and Prison Brotherhood of Bikers. A review of the sentences of gang members within the New Jersey Department of Corrections reveals that most gang inmates serve five years or less before returning to the community. With such relatively short prison terms, it is imperative that the department shares the gang organization, rank structure, codes affiliation and membership of incarcerated gang members with outside law enforcement entities, including municipal and state, to safeguard the community upon release of these inmates.

In 1996 the NJDOC initiated the Combined Law Enforcement Intelligence Committee or CLIC, which is comprised of investigators and detectives from multiple agencies throughout

Solitary Confinement Helps Control Gangs

The "gang war" between the Bloods and the Hispanic inmates (Latin Kings and Netas) was in full swing in 1996 when the department began to build the first of four thousand eight hundred "beds" in maximum security cells. These were the first maximum security cells that had been built in the state in over ten years. It was called "right sizing" the prison population. To put inmates who needed to be classified maximum security in maximum security prisons. Or inmates with long term disciplinary confinement sentences into disciplinary cells. . . . The department was finally getting the cell space to lock up a lot of the troublemakers. . . .

It has been my experience that cells have been the number one project that the state embarked on that reduced violence and made the gangs easier to control. As then Commissioner Goord alluded to in April 2003, the department created the cell space to lock up the troublemaking inmates and they knew it. Now troublemaking gang members either stay locked up in disciplinary confinement . . . or they have conformed to the rules and regulations of the department and live relatively trouble free in general population.

John Hancock,
"Combating Gang Activity in Prison,"
March 24, 2008. www.corrections.com.

the state. Monthly meetings are convened with federal, state, regional, county and municipal law enforcement agencies, with but one objective—sharing information on gangs and their members. Lists of identified inmates and aliases are distributed, as is a monthly bulletin that highlights new tattoos, codes, graffiti, statewide trends, identification statistics and incident reports. Moreover, this committee has created a network of professionals who can contact one another outside of the meetings to ascertain the whereabouts and identities of gangs in the community.

The Gang Reduction and Aggressive Supervised Parole Plan

Personnel from the New Jersey State Police Street Gang Unit (SGU), the New Jersey Department of Corrections, and the New Jersey Division of Parole have developed an interagency plan called Gang Reduction & Aggressive Supervised Parole (GRASP,) which will significantly benefit the work of each agency related to street gangs in urban venues.

Under this program, GRASP participants aggressively target gang member parolees to ensure compliance with the terms of parole (including non-association with gang members).

A GRASP team consisting of SGU members, NJDOC investigators, and parole officers, makes unannounced home visits and interviews at parole offices with parolees who were identified during their incarceration in NJDOC facilities as members of one of seven recognized gangs/Security Threat Groups.

Such concentrated efforts, from three law enforcement entities, produce an added safeguard to our citizens, and discourage gang violence and the subsequent victimization.

Gang Awareness and Prevention

While the New Jersey Department of Corrections has made gang management and intelligence sharing a priority, the department has set yet another—zero growth of the gang population. The Gang Awareness and Prevention Program—GAPP was created to meet this goal. Perhaps Commissioner Devon Brown says it best: "The Gang Awareness and Prevention Program brings inmates who have renounced their gang membership into schools and other civic venues to discuss the horrors and violence associated with gang membership and the often deadly fate that awaits gang bangers. It is a testament to the effectiveness of the Security Threat Group Management Unit that so many gang members have graduated from the program and renounced their gang affiliation, thereby creating a safer environment for staff in the prisons.

"In addition, all of New Jersey's citizens benefit by the approach to gangs, as the recidivism rate is appreciably lower for those inmates who graduate from the STGMU program," he continued. "If even one youngster attending a GAPP presentation heeds the admonitions of the reformed gang member, our mission to prevent crime is crowned with success."

Gang Awareness at Home and at School

Parents and educators should be concerned if they notice any of the following:

- Negative behavior changes

- Drop in grades

- Change in attitude toward authority

- Drug or alcohol use

- Gang graffiti

- Photos of gang members on display

- The appearance of gang names, slogans and insignias inscribed on belongings

- Wearing only gang colors (red for Bloods, blue for Crips)

- Tattoos

- Flashing gang signs to others

The gang recruitment process plays out in urban and suburban areas throughout the state every day. The child who feels unloved, who receives little or no parental supervision or who has low self-esteem will be a target for the gang recruiter.

With a centralized database that is updated daily, in-depth academy training, monthly intelligence meetings and institutional training, the New Jersey Department of Corrections, under the leadership of Commissioner Devon Brown, has addressed the problem of gangs in prisons aggressively, proactively, and with a sense of urgency that reflects a commitment to public safety, both in and out of the prison setting. The fact that local, state, and federal agencies have reached out to the NJDOC for assistance in the identification and control of gangs lends credence to this assessment. As has often been proven true, imitation is the sincerest form of flattery. In this respect, numerous other states have looked to model New Jersey's approach to prison management of gangs. Most recently, North Carolina has replicated the NJDOC's STGMU, with Maryland looking to follow suit in the very near future. "In essence, safer behind bars for our officers, safer on the street for our citizens," Commissioner Brown says.

Periodical Bibliography

The following articles have been selected to supplement the diverse views presented in this chapter.

Martin Bentham   "New Nickname or Slang? How to Spot If Your Child Is in a Gang," *Evening Standard*, September 2, 2008.

Ed Caesar   "Are Rap Artists Responsible for the Explosion of Gang Culture? The Big Question," *The Independent*, August 10, 2007.

Jill Carroll   "In Cairo, Hordes of Street Kids, but No Longer Ignored," *Christian Science Monitor*, January 31, 2008.

Laura Clout   "Gang Culture Is Replacing Family Life, Says Police Chief," *Daily Telegraph*, July 2, 2008.

Pippa Crerar   "Jack Straw Links Absent Fathers to Gang Violence," *Evening Standard*, August 21, 2007.

Veronique Dupere   "Affiliation to Youth Gangs During Adolescence: The Interaction Between Childhood Psychopathic Tendencies and Neighborhood Disadvantage," *Journal of Abnormal Child Psychology*, December 2007.

Gary Mason   "With Love from Prison: Guatemala's Gangs," *Globe and Mail*, January 7, 2008.

Alastair McIndoe   "Rap Brings Together Rival Gangs in Manila Slums," *The Straits Times*, December 11, 2007.

Terrance J. Taylor   "Youth Gang Membership and Serious Violent Victimization: The Importance of Lifestyles and Routine," *Journal of Interpersonal Violence*, October 2008.

Alan Travis   "Seeking Solitary: Prison Gang Wars Force Fearful Inmates to Plead for Segregation," *The Guardian*, February 18, 2008.

What Should Be Done to Prevent Gangs?

Chapter Preface

Gang prevention is often discussed as a problem requiring complex bureaucratic intervention: retraining law enforcement officials; retooling the way the criminal justice system responds to juvenile offenders; or large-scale gang prevention programs. Can merely educating the community about gangs help prevent gangs in our communities?

The California attorney general's Web site puts education at the top of a list of actions communities can take against gangs. U.S. Representative Elijah E. Cummings describes how he has participated in gang prevention efforts in Maryland: "In my Congressional District, I have teamed up with Mr. Frank Clark, the Director of Gang Intervention and Investigation for the Maryland Department of Juvenile Services, to hold three gang prevention summits. Mr. Clark gives an excellent presentation for parents, teachers, and other members of the community to educate them about the signs and language of gang activity to make sure that we do not mistakenly dismiss dangerous communication from our children as harmless or useless slang."

Police departments also recognize the importance of community education in preventing gangs from taking root in communities. The police department of Freeport, New York, has made community education a central part of its anti-gang efforts, as Chief Michael Woodward explained to the House of Representative's Subcommittee on Healthy Families and Communities in June of 2007: "The immediate focus of the Freeport Police Department's efforts to mitigate gang recruitment was a Gang Awareness Suppression and Prevention Program (GASPP). The demographics of the street gang population encompass a broad spectrum of race, ethnicity, gender and age and the program provides gang related information to parents, community members, school staffs, and the work force in an effort to reduce gang recruitment."

Other organizations such as the East Coast Gang Investigators Association (ECGIA) hold such a strong belief in the importance of community education in the effort to stop the development of gangs that they have made community education their sole mission. The purpose of ECGIA is "working to educate the communities and those entrusted to work with our youth about gangs." They argue further that "the lack of quality information and the misinformation that is available to the public greatly increases the gangs' ability to succeed in their criminal endeavors and to recruit our children into the gangster lifestyle."

Education is just one part of many communities' efforts to stop gangs. In the following viewpoints the authors consider what can be done to prevent gangs. Efforts to stop gangs range from education, to the creation of legislation, to community programs.

> *"Legislators clearly are coming together to find ways to address the disturbing increase in gang violence."*

State Lawmakers Are Helping to Prevent Gangs

Sarah Hammond

In the following viewpoint, Sarah Hammond describes the measures state lawmakers are taking to curb the growing gang problem. She explains that lawmakers believe that the battle against gangs has to involve the family as well as heavier prison penalties. Sarah Hammond reports on juvenile justice issues for the National Conference of State Legislatures.

As you read, consider the following questions:

1. What are the three components of the Washington State Anti-Gang Act?
2. Why, according to Representative Christopher Hurst, can we not just "arrest our way out of the problem"?
3. What do parents of some gang members in California learn in their violence prevention classes?

Sarah Hammond, "Gang Busters: States Respond to Rising Gang Violence," *State Legislatures*, June 2008, pp. 20–21. Copyright © 2008 National Conference of State Legislatures. Reproduced by permission.

Early this year in Los Angeles, 17-year-old Jamiel Andre Shaw, a high school football star, was walking down the street and talking on his cell phone to his girlfriend when someone came up and asked what gang he was in. When he didn't answer, he was shot to death.

Shaw's death is just one example of the thousands of victims killed each year in gang-related crimes across the county. From Boston to Los Angeles, across the Midwest and down to Georgia and Florida, gang activity and violence is on the rise. It's also deadlier than ever, thanks to drugs and guns.

While it was once only an inner-city problem, today gangs have spread nationwide to suburbs, small towns and Native American reservations. And they draw new members from all walks of life.

According to the FBI [Federal Bureau of Investigation], there are now more than 30,000 different gangs across America with some 800,000 members. They're in all 50 states and the U.S. territories.

Why Do Kids Join?

The FBI defines a gang as "a group of three or more individuals bonded together by race, national origin, culture or territory, who associate on a continual basis for the purpose of committing criminal acts." Many gangs are a product of a specific neighborhood or locale, but some gangs have established national franchises far from their home base.

Kids join gangs for protection and emotional and social support. Mostly, gangs start up in unstable, poor neighborhoods. Broken homes, violent parents and family members, and access to drugs all play a part. At-risk and delinquent youths are usually the same kids who end up in gangs. Sometimes, membership in a certain gang is a family tradition. Kids join the gang that their father, brother or cousins joined before them.

| | | Indictments & | | |
Year	Complaints	Informations	Arrests	Convictions
2001	1,143	2,181	3,999	2,168
2002	1,024	1,951	3,512	1,964
2003	826	1,971	3,837	1,698
2004	980	2,183	4,162	1,773
2005	1,191	2,540	4,745	1,700
2006	1,421	2,695	5,537	2,199
Totals	6,585	13,521	25,792	11,502

Violent Gang Safe Street Task Force Accomplishments

TAKEN FROM: Federal Bureau of Investigation.

Gangs have more money and power than in recent decades, making them attractive to younger children who see powerful members driving fancy cars and sporting fancy guns. The richer gangs become, the more competitive they are in their recruitment.

There's no denying that the thriving meth trade has accounted for some of the recent increase in gang activity. For decades, homemade methamphetamine was a small-time drug. Meth "cooks" worked in home kitchens, making a few ounces for themselves or to sell through motorcycle gangs. But tough legislation passed in recent years made pseudoephedrine [an ingredient of methamphetamine] harder to get and shut down numerous meth labs. With meth cooks out of the way, Mexican drug cartels are targeting street gangs, especially on the West Coast and in Arizona, to distribute the deadly and highly addictive drug.

An Example from Washington State

As gang crime and violence have increased, state lawmakers have stiffened sentences for gang members and created penal ties for those who recruit minors into gangs. They have passed laws to develop programs to help prevent youths at risk from getting involved with gangs.

That is precisely what Washington state is doing because "gangs are on the rise in every corner of the state," says Representative Christopher Hurst, a retired police detective with 25 years on the job and sponsor of a comprehensive new law, the Anti-Gang Act.

Hurst says the law is the product of a bipartisan task force that toured the state, taking testimony from citizens, police officers, prosecutors and community activists. It funds three core components for dealing with gangs:

- Prevention—stopping kids from being recruited into gangs in the first place.

- Intervention—rescuing teenagers from gang membership.

- Suppression—busting up gangs, especially by going after the adults who recruit children.

"Police and prosecutors told us that we can't arrest our way out of the gang problem," Hurst says. "The older gang members will just recruit more kids. We need a comprehensive attack to fight the growth of gangs, and that's what this law is about."

The Washington law penalizes adults who recruit minors to commit crimes. Arizona and New Jersey are also putting new penalties in place that make it a crime to solicit or recruit a minor into a gang.

What California Is Doing

Other recent actions include a 2007 California law that requires parents of some gang members to take violence prevention classes, patterned after those that drivers take when they violate traffic laws. They must pay for the classes themselves.

"I was startled with the overwhelming support of both Democrats and Republicans for this legislation," says its sponsor, Assemblyman Tony Mendoza, a former elementary school teacher in East Los Angeles.

Research indicates that parents play a key role in keeping young people out of gangs, Mendoza says. Negative influences within the family can increase the risk that a child will join a gang.

"We have to help parents take control of their children," says Mendoza. "There are many parents who want to, but just don't know how."

The parenting classes focus on how to recognize signs that a child has joined a gang or is involved in drugs; how to communicate with teens; and how to find alcohol and drug abuse treatment, educational programs, recreational activities and job training. The classes also educate parents about the legal system.

"There are parents whose own alcohol or drug dependencies are so severe that they themselves are involved with gangs," says Mendoza. "We have to break the cycle of gang activity in families to stop the revolving door of juvenile gang members going in and out of jail."

The California Legislature also established the Office of Gang and Youth Violence Policy to develop ways to prevent gang violence and youth involvement. And a new law in Illinois now funds gang resistance education and training in all grades, elementary through high school.

Other States Fight Back

Lawmakers are also going after graffiti that claims and defines a gang's territory with paintings of its name or symbol. Graffiti sends a mindless message of turf and machismo. Arizona and Hawaii created new penalties for property damage from graffiti. Tennessee makes parents responsible when a juvenile vandalizes property and requires them to clean the damage or pay for its repair. Texas requires the juvenile offender to make restitution to the owner of the defaced property.

Legislators clearly are coming together to find ways to address the disturbing increase in gang violence.

"The time is now to fight back," says Hurst. "We need to prevent gangs from terrorizing communities and, first and foremost, stop them from recruiting innocent kids into their dead-end life."

| "The official response to an emerging gang problem is rarely based on a solid understanding of gang issues or a coherent theory of what an intervention should accomplish."

Policy Makers and Police Do Not Help Prevent Gangs

Judith Greene and Kevin Pranis

In the following viewpoint, the authors claim that many policies and programs intended to combat gangs are not well planned or carefully carried out, and are thus ineffective. According to their analysis, police gang task forces are usually created when a gang problem is identified, but those task forces do not have enough support from the rest of the police department, often have unclear missions, and sometimes have problems with corruption. Judith Greene is a criminal justice policy analyst and a founding partner in Justice Strategies, a resource clearinghouse on prison and law enforcement policy. Kevin Pranis is a researcher and policy analyst.

Judith Greene and Kevin Pranis, "Gang Wars: The Failure of Enforcement Tactics and the Need for Effective Public Safety Strategies," Justice Policy Institute, July 17, 2007, pp. 68–96. Reproduced by permission.

As you read, consider the following questions:

1. According to the authors, what do law enforcement officials often define as the only objective of an anti-gang effort? Do the authors agree with that strategy?
2. What problem do the authors see with police efforts to target gang leaders?
3. What do most police gang units do, according to a study cited by the authors?

When the existence of a gang problem has been announced or acknowledged by public officials, the conversation generally turns to how law enforcement should solve it. The following are fairly typical policy responses to the emergence of a gang problem:

1. Form a specialized gang unit within the police department if one does not already exist.
2. Launch a crackdown in high-crime neighborhoods by adding police patrols, aggressively enforcing public ordinances, and using every available opportunity to stop and question local residents.
3. Target alleged gang "leaders" and "hard-core" gang members for heightened surveillance and stiff criminal justice sanctions.

Other policy makers may propose adoption of a fourth option—a "balanced" approach that combines the gang enforcement tactics described here with provision of services and supports to gang members and gang-afflicted communities. The choice of a gang enforcement strategy is frequently based on political and institutional considerations. Officials seek strategies that let the public know they are "doing something" about the problem without requiring fundamental changes in the police department's operations.

The official response to an emerging gang problem is rarely based on a solid understanding of gang issues or a coherent theory of what an intervention should accomplish. The hysteria that greets the sudden emergence of a gang problem creates a poor atmosphere for considering the questions that will determine the success or failure of a gang control strategy: What are its *objectives*? Whom will it *target*? And what *effect* will the initiative have on the targets in order to achieve the objectives?

What Are the Objectives?

The objectives of a gang control effort depend on whether the problem is defined as gang violence, gang crime, or the gangs' very existence. Law enforcement officials often take the public position that gangs must be eradicated. In the words of Captain Ray Peavy, who heads the Los Angeles sheriff's homicide bureau, "Everyone says: 'What are we going to do about the gang problem?' It's the same thing you do about cockroaches or insects; you get someone in there to do whatever they can do to get rid of those creatures."

Others take a different perspective on what gang control efforts can, or should, set out to accomplish. As a representative of one urban community development corporation told a researcher, "The problem is not to get kids out of gangs but the behavior. If crime goes down, if young people are doing well, that's successful." Some law enforcement officers also acknowledge—usually in private—that their goal is not to eliminate gang *membership* but to reduce levels of gang *crime* and *violence*.

Who Is the Target?

The second important question for gang control efforts is whom to target. On one hand, an initiative may elect to target "leaders" or "hard-core" members who are believed to be the driving force behind gang crime. On the other hand, the initiative may target "fringe" members or even nonmembers whom policy makers believe can more easily be enticed or deterred from gang activity.

The most appropriate target depends on one's theory about how gangs operate. Some law enforcement officials subscribe to the view that gangs can be eliminated or at least neutralized by removing their leadership ("cutting the head off the snake"). Others argue that gang leadership is fluid, and that gangs—like the mythical hydra—are capable of growing new heads faster than law enforcement can decapitate them. Some contend that so-called "hard-core" members should be targeted because they do (and suffer) the most damage. But others believe that a focus on newer and more marginal members will not only save more youth but also limit gangs' ability to reproduce themselves over time.

If drive-by shootings and other spectacular acts of gang violence are committed by younger members at the behest of leaders, then it is possible—although not certain—that removing the leaders from the community might reduce violence. If, on the other hand, drive-bys and other acts of violence are initiated by younger and more volatile members with poor impulse control and a desire to "prove" themselves, then removing leaders will do nothing to quell the violence.

What Effect Will the Initiative Have?

The third critical question for gang control efforts is what effects they are intended to have on the targets. A gang control initiative may set out to *incapacitate* gang members who are deemed too dangerous to remain on the street due to their role in the gang or their personal involvement in crime and violence. An initiative may also seek to use "carrots" or "sticks" to *persuade* individuals to change behaviors ranging from gang membership to gun violence. Finally, a gang control initiative may try to *disrupt* gang activities by making it impossible for individuals or the group as a whole to function normally.

Boston's Operation Ceasefire is an example of a gang control effort with clear objectives, targets, and intended effects.

The architects of Operation Ceasefire set *reducing gun violence* as the principal objective and stuck with that objective throughout the life of the project. They developed a strategy that was designed to *persuade* both *hard-core* and *fringe* youth gang members to stop engaging in acts of retaliatory violence.

Targeted youth were told that further acts of violence would place them and their gangs under heightened law enforcement scrutiny; they were offered supports and services designed to facilitate the transition from gang activities to other activities. Police also conducted saturation patrols and prosecuted targeted gang leaders, but these actions were considered components of the main "lever-pulling" strategy rather than competing strategies.

The conceptual clarity that characterized Operation Ceasefire is rare among gang control efforts. Few initiatives have proved capable of orienting their activities around realistic, measurable public safety objectives. And most are unable to articulate a viable theory of how gang control activities will have the intended effect on their targets. Gang enforcement efforts mounted in response to public concerns about gang and gun *violence* have driven up arrests for *nonviolent* offenses with no reduction in violence. Gang intervention programs that were intended to target active members wind up serving nonmembers because the staff is unwilling to work with "that kind of kid." Conceptual clarity is no guarantee of success. The failure of efforts to replicate the Ceasefire model in Los Angeles and Indianapolis cast doubt on the underlying theory of "lever pulling" and deterrence "retailing." But such clarity does make it easier to evaluate and debate competing proposals.

Problems of Gang Enforcement Efforts

Further, the thrust of most gang enforcement efforts runs counter to what is known about gangs and gang members,

Change in crime (gang and nongang) associated with St. Louis Anti-Gang Initiative

	Target neighborhoods		Control neighborhoods	
Crime category	College Hill	Fairground Park	O'Fallon Park	Hyde park
Murder	NS	NS	NS	NS
Robbery	NS	NS	NS	NS
Robbery—weapon	NS	NS	NS	NS
Robbery—no weapon	NS	-35.7%	NS	+52.6%
Assault	NS	NS	+64.0%	NS
Gun assault	NS	NS	NS	NS
Person crime	NS	NS	NS	NS
Property crime	NS	NS	NS	NS
Index crime	NS	NS	NS	NS

Note: NS Statistically nonsignificant

TAKEN FROM: Judith Greene and Kevin Pranis, "Gang wars", *The Failure of Enforcement Tactics and the Need for Effective Public Safety Strategies*, "Justice Policy Institute, July 17, 2007.

rendering the efforts ineffectual if not counterproductive. Police officials make much of targeting reputed "leaders" while ignoring the fact that most gangs do not need leaders to function (not to mention the risk that removal of leaders will increase violence by destabilizing the gang and removing constraints on internal conflict). Research on the dynamics of gang membership indicates that suppression tactics intended to make youth "think twice" about gang involvement may instead reinforce gang cohesion, elevating the gang's importance and reinforcing an "us versus them" mentality. Finally, the incarceration of gang members is often considered a measure of success, even though prison tends to solidify gang involvement and weaken an individual's capacity to live a gang- and crime-free life.

It is easy to provide anecdotal evidence for the effectiveness of any one of these strategies: media reports are full of stories about cities where crime goes up, a crackdown is launched, and crime goes down. But a review of research on the implementation of gang enforcement strategies—ranging from neighborhood-based suppression to the U.S. Justice Department Office of Juvenile Justice and Delinquency Prevention's Comprehensive Gang Program Model—provides little reason for optimism. Findings from investigations of gang enforcement efforts in 17 jurisdictions over the past two decades yield few examples of success, and many examples of failure.

The problems highlighted in the research include:

- Lack of correspondence between the problem, typically lethal and/or serious violence, and a law enforcement response that targets low-level, nonviolent misbehavior.

- Resistance on the part of key agency personnel to collaboration or implementation of the strategy as designed.

- Evidence that the intervention had no effect or a negative effect on crime and violence.

- A tendency for any reductions in crime or violence to evaporate quickly, often before the end of the intervention period.

- Poorly designed evaluations that make it impossible to draw any conclusions about the effect of an intervention.

- Failure of replication efforts to achieve results comparable to those of pilot programs.

- Severe power and resources imbalances between law enforcement and community partners that hamper the implementation of "balanced" gang control initiatives.

The following sections describe common gang enforcement strategies and explore findings of program evaluations from 17 jurisdictions.

The Rise of Police Gang Units

Over the past decade and a half, we have witnessed a proliferation within law enforcement agencies of specialized units that focus on gang enforcement. The formation of a gang unit is often viewed as a rational response to an emerging gang threat. But researchers have concluded that gang units are more often formed in response to pressure on police to "do something," or as a way to secure additional resources for the agency. Once gang units are launched, the experts find they often become isolated from the rest of the department, a development that can render them ineffective or even facilitate corruption.

Roughly half of local law enforcement agencies with 100 or more sworn officers maintain special gang units, according to a 1999 survey, including 56 percent of municipal police departments, 50 percent of sheriff's departments, and 43 percent of county police agencies. In 2003 Charles Katz and Vincent Webb [authors of *Policing Gangs in America*] estimated that the total number of police gang units (including state police agencies) stood at 360, most of which (85 percent) were no more than 10 years old. . . .

What Gang Units Do

It should be no surprise that gang units whose formation was precipitated by external pressures or opportunities rather than a coherent law enforcement strategy would have difficulty establishing a role within the agency. Katz found that "once the gang unit was created it was often required to incorporate competing ideas and beliefs into its organizational structure and operational strategy to communicate an image of operational effectiveness when it otherwise was unable to demonstrate success."

Katz and Webb found that most gang units gravitated toward intelligence-gathering and enforcement/suppression activities while devoting less attention to investigations and very little to prevention. The authors' conclusions on the operation of gang units are not encouraging. The majority of the police departments they studied lacked formal mechanisms to monitor gang unit officers and hold them accountable for job performance.

No Central Leadership

The gang units tended to engage in "buffet-style policing," accepting only cases that involved high-profile crimes such as homicides, drive-by shootings, and aggravated assaults. Priorities were not set by a well-articulated vision of the unit's mission but instead were determined by a "unique workgroup subculture . . . that reflected internally shared beliefs about the nature of the local gang problem and the appropriate response to that problem." The chief of one police department admitted to the researchers that he had "little understanding of what the gang unit did or how it operated."

The absence of strong departmental oversight and the physical separation of gang units from the rest of the police force—three of four units operated from "secret" off-site facilities that were known only to gang unit officers—contributed to a "decoupling [that] led gang unit officers to isolate themselves from the rest of the police organization and from the community and its citizens." Although gang units are supposed to afford an opportunity for officers to develop specialized expertise, the authors found that the officers were poorly trained and had little direct exposure to gang members: an average of just one to three contacts per eight hours worked.

Gang unit officers "rarely sought citizen input" or partnerships with community organizations, according to the researchers: "None of the gang unit officers in any of the study sites appeared to value information that *non*-criminal justice agencies might provide, nor did they recognize potential value in sharing their own information and knowledge with non-criminal justice personnel." Gang units appeared instead to have adopted a Spy vs. Spy worldview that extended to their own departments. Some gang officers professed that "regular precinct stations or police headquarters were subject to penetration by gangs, purportedly rendering intelligence files vulnerable to destruction and manipulation."

Problems with the Isolation of Gang Units

Given the isolation of gang units from their departments and their communities, it is not surprising that interview participants "were hard-pressed to offer specific evidence of the units' effectiveness" and "rarely commented on the gang units' impact on the amelioration of local gang problems." Lack of confidence in the gang units' effectiveness was most pronounced on the topic of suppression. The researchers found that "almost no one other than the gang unit officers themselves seemed to believe that gang unit suppression efforts were effective at reducing the communities' gang problems."

The isolation of gang units from host agencies and their tendency to form tight-knit subcultures—not entirely unlike those of gangs—also contributes to a disturbingly high incidence of corruption and other misconduct. The Los Angeles Police Department's Rampart scandal is only the most famous example of a gang unit gone bad. Katz and Webb cite several other places where police gang units have drawn attention for aggressive tactics and misconduct, including Las Vegas, where two gang unit officers participated in a drive-by shooting of alleged gang members; Chicago, where gang unit officers worked with local gangs to import cocaine from Miami; and

Houston, where gang task force officers were found to routinely engage in unauthorized use of confidential informants, warrantless searches, and firing weapons at unarmed citizens.

Katz and Webb conclude by recommending that police departments with gang units take steps to make them more effective, including better integrating gang units into the department's patrol and investigative functions; strengthening managerial controls and accountability; and incorporating community policing strategies. But their research findings also suggest that police officials should reconsider whether gang units are an effective law enforcement tool or a potentially dangerous distraction from the real work at hand.

"The police say the murdered teenager was the leader of the Pretty Boy Family, which they describe as a subdivision, or 'set,' of the Bloods gang. But those who knew Mr. McFarland and are familiar with the Pretty Boy Family described it as a tight group of friends who like to dance and hang out, not a gang."

Police Do Not Effectively Combat Gangs

Trymaine Lee

In the following viewpoint, Trymaine Lee reports on an incident in which a large group of adolescents were arrested because they were misidentified by police as gang members. The author suggests that police may have picked up this group of teenagers not because of anything they did, but to gather information for their investigation into a local gang. Lee is a writer and blogger for The New York Times.

As you read, consider the following questions:

1. What evidence is given that these arrests were part of a carefully planned effort on the part of the police?

Trymaine Lee, "In the Details of a Mass Arrest, Two Versions, Worlds Apart," *The New York Times*, June 24, 2007. Reproduced by permission.

2. What event was the catalyst for these arrests?

3. What do many of those who were arrested say they were questioned about by police?

The police officers hopped from their vans and cars with shouts of "Hands up," "Don't move," and "Get on the ground." Someone in the crowd of young people yelled, "Nobody run"—and nobody did, witnesses said. The teenagers were frisked, forced up against a fence or a wall, or pushed to the asphalt.

Those watching said the mood was almost subdued as the handcuffs went on, the loudest sound the whir of a television news helicopter hovering above. "None of us understood what was going on," said Dana Hollis, whose teenage daughter was arrested. "Everything just happened so fast."

Thirty-two young people, the youngest 13, were arrested the afternoon of May 21 [2007] in Bushwick, Brooklyn. They had been walking as a group to the subway, which they planned to take to Coney Island for the wake [part of the funeral customs of some cultures] of Donnell McFarland, 18, who had been fatally shot a week earlier.

Two Different Stories

The police, already fearing retaliatory violence, say the teenagers were exchanging gang signs, wearing T-shirts with a gang name and bounding atop cars when they were arrested. Parents and teachers of the group and witnesses said that they were no more boisterous than any group of teenagers would be in similar circumstances, and that they did not see any youths atop cars.

The charges are misdemeanors: unlawful assembly and disorderly conduct. No drugs or weapons were found, and there were no injuries to those arrested or to the police. The officers did not draw their guns. Yet this roundup of Brooklyn teenagers and young people has gotten widespread attention.

Interviews with those arrested, their parents, witnesses who did not know the teenagers, as well as accounts provided by the Police Department and the Brooklyn district attorney, provided contradictory versions of events. But they correspond in one aspect: The arrests were part of a police operation that unfolded with precision.

The Arrests

Undercover officers circled in unmarked cars; a police captain monitored the teenagers gathering; and blue-and-white vans and buses cut off Putnam Avenue in both directions at a key moment, trapping the teenagers less than a block into their journey.

"Once the kids hit Irving, the police came from everywhere," said Lisa Guerrero, 52, who lives nearby and saw the group gather and head up the block. "I was like: 'What happened? Why is this happening?'"

Paul J. Browne, the Police Department's chief spokesman, said, "The police were being responsive to community leaders who warned that the group was poised for trouble after a week of murder, shootings and fistfights between two rival gang factions in Bushwick."

The Murder of Donnell McFarland

On May 15 [2007], Mr. McFarland was shot in the head at Linden Street and Knickerbocker Avenue by James Kelly, 16, the police said. Mr. Kelly was soon arrested and charged with murder and criminal possession of a weapon. Friends of both said the shooting was the climax in a string of violent events involving Mr. Kelly, a onetime friend of Mr. McFarland's turned enemy.

The shot echoed for blocks.

"We were on the basketball court, and we all kind of froze," said Asher Callender, 19. Someone ran into the park, crying, using Mr. McFarland's nickname: "They killed Freshh."

Police Say They Can't Fight Gangs Alone

"Suppression [enforcement] alone, that doesn't work," said [Sergeant] Juan Aguilar of the [Washington] D.C. police. "That's only a Band-Aid. You've got to get to the root of the problem. It's social."

Similar sentiments were expressed by officials in [nearby] Arlington and Fairfax [Virginia] counties, who said their police departments work closely with a variety of social service providers. In 2005, after a spate of gang violence in Northern Virginia, Fairfax launched a Coordinating Council on Gang Prevention and required several county service providers to participate.

Last year, Arlington launched its "Attention to Prevention" initiative to provide mentoring, leadership training and tutoring for youths. Police spokesman John Lisle said, "It's clear to us, to reduce the impact of gangs, it's not just a matter of locking people up."

Tom Jackman, Washington Post, *July 18, 2007.*

The police say the murdered teenager was the leader of the Pretty Boy Family, which they describe as a subdivision, or "set," of the Bloods gang. But those who knew Mr. McFarland and are familiar with the Pretty Boy Family described it as a tight group of friends who like to dance and hang out, not a gang. The police say the Pretty Boy Family had been at odds with James Kelly's gang, the Linden Street Bloods, another Bloods subdivision, for some time. Both sets frequent the Hope Gardens housing project.

The Response to McFarland's Death

Word of Mr. McFarland's death spread from the neighborhood streets into neighborhood schools.

"I didn't have a single class that whole week where I didn't have two or three people in my class crying," said Tabari Bomani, a social studies teacher and college counselor at Bushwick Community High School, where many students knew Mr. McFarland. Dozens of them met with grief counselors, school officials said.

Mr. McFarland's wake was set for the following Monday at a funeral home in Coney Island. Officials at the Bushwick high school allowed students to sign out for the day if parents signed a permission slip.

Mr. Callender said that many students wanted to attend, but that he was one of the few who knew the way to the funeral home. So he spread the word: Meet at Putnam Park between noon and 12:30 the day of the wake, May 21 [2007]. They would gather, walk up Putnam, and head for the subway station.

A Series of Attacks

Meanwhile, police were connecting the dots in a yearlong investigation into the Pretty Boy Family and a recent rash of gang violence.

The police said a Pretty Boy Family member was shot in the foot two weeks before Mr. McFarland's death. Later, they said, there was a confrontation between William Gonzalez, who had been feuding with Mr. McFarland, and a man they believed belonged to the Pretty Boy Family.

The same day, Jakai King, whom the police described as a member of the Linden Street Bloods, was attacked by members of the Pretty Boy Family, the police said. Two days later, they said, he was attacked again, this time stripped down to his underwear and sent running down the street.

It was in this atmosphere of attacks and revenge, Mr. Browne said, that the police received reports that a gang would be "mustering at the park" the day of the wake and that there would be violence. Community leaders warned the police in the 83rd Precinct in Bushwick and the 60th Precinct in Coney Island that Mr. McFarland's rivals had said that they would shoot anyone wearing a T-shirt memorializing him.

What the Students Did

Ms. Hollis, 40, her 15-year-old daughter and two of her nieces joined Donna Seabury and her two daughters, 12 and 16, at the park. Mr. Callender said he went to the school that morning to retrieve the school permission slip he left with the assistant principal. He then headed to the park. He was early, one of the first students to arrive. His friends slowly trickled in.

The teenagers were to wear similar T-shirts, bearing Mr. McFarland's picture and words like "R.I.P. Freshh," to the wake.

Luis Pacheco, 18, said he went to the print shop that morning to pick up his $14 T-shirt. After meeting a friend, they went to the park. It was just about 12:30 p.m.

Others recounted similar stories: rushing to school to get slips, waiting for their parents to walk with them to the park, meeting friends to travel together.

Zezza Anderson, 18, said teenagers sat in small groups or off by themselves. "Everyone's sad. We're sad; we're grieving," Mr. Anderson said. "No one was being rowdy. Just chilling, waiting for everyone to show up. We're trying to make sure we don't leave anybody behind."

Just after 1 p.m. the students walked from the handball courts to the macadam path that leads to the street.

What the Police Did

Capt. Scott Henderson, of the 83rd Precinct, was one of the officers doing surveillance. In his report, he wrote that the teenagers greeted one another with gang hand signs, wore gang bandannas and shirts with a gang name on them, and gathered near a wall covered with gang slogans. Mr. Browne said last week that since they believed Mr. McFarland was in a gang, the police considered "Freshh" a gang name.

The police said the group then left the park and took over Putnam Avenue, stopping traffic, frightening pedestrians and hopping onto parked cars. "It's when he sees that group grow in size and start walking on cars and forcing others to go into the street is when he called for the arrests," Mr. Browne said of the captain. "It's not like they had a plan where they were going to go to the park and arrest people."

What Witnesses Saw

Some witnesses, including some parents, said the teenagers were behaving peacefully. The Brooklyn district attorney's office said witnesses saw unruly behavior, including walking on cars, but Charles J. Hynes, the district attorney, would not provide specifics of those accounts.

Several owners of cars that were parked on the block said they did not notice any damage to their vehicles afterward.

Hector Polonia, 52, was sweeping the sidewalk in front of United Cleaners, where he works as manager, on Irving Avenue near Putnam, when he saw the group crossing Putnam. Then he saw the police move in. "They weren't making any noise or anything," Mr. Polonia said. "They were acting like a normal bunch of teenagers."

Ms. Guerrero was sitting in Putnam Park. "They didn't get on any cars," she said of the teenagers.

The Interrogations

Those under 16 were quickly released. The six female mourners in the group were given summonses for disorderly conduct. The remaining young men were run through the system, charged with disorderly conduct and unlawful assembly. Most remained in jail overnight, some as long as 36 hours.

"They seemed more interested in asking us questions about the murder than telling us why we were arrested," Mr. Callender said. "They just kept asking us stuff like, 'Who has the guns?' and 'Who is going to strike next?' But they were giving me information about people that I didn't even know. They knew more than we did."

Several of the teenagers said they were interrogated about the Pretty Boy Family. Some said the police pulled out a big black binder labeled "P.B.F." with photos of people from the neighborhood.

"At first I thought they were going to question us, then let us go," said Mr. Pacheco. "But then I could see the sun going down from my cell. I got upset. And people were crying. Some people were throwing up."

The last members of the group were released on May 23 [2007]. The next day, a news conference was held at the headquarters of Make the Road by Walking, a community rights organization in Bushwick.

More than 50 students, including many of those who were arrested, demanded an apology from the Police Department.

The district attorney has offered to give those arrested community service assignments in return for guilty pleas. So far, none have accepted.

"The ... gang youth was helped to find a job, complete high school, or pursue further education."

Gang Prevention Programs That Offer Alternatives to Youth Will Decrease Gang Activity

Irving A. Spergel

In the following viewpoint, author Irving A. Spergel describes a gang intervention project that he coordinated for four years in Chicago beginning in 1992. The project was created in response to the critique that other gang intervention programs had claimed successes but without any empirical evidence—that is to say, actual field-tested evidence—to support those claims. A key feature of this project was the use of former gang members as outreach youth workers. Irving A. Spergel is a retired professor at the School of Social Service Administration at the University of Chicago.

Irving A. Spergel, *Reducing Youth Gang Violence: The Little Village Gang Project in Chicago.* Lanham, MD: AltaMira Press, 2007, pp. 343–355. Copyright © 2007 AltaMira Press. All rights reserved. Reproduced by permission of Rowman & Littlefield.

As you read, consider the following questions:

1. What were the responsibilities of outreach youth workers in the gang intervention project?

2. What changes did researchers find in the perceptions of youth from the two gangs when interviewed during the project?

3. What changes did researchers find in the number of offenses committed by gang members participating in the project?

The key questions this book [*Reducing Youth Gang Violence*] has tried to answer are how the Little Village Gang Violence Reduction Project developed, what its model of a comprehensive, interdisciplinary community approach was, and to what extent the project was successful in reducing violence of gang youth. The model stressed the integration of several program strategies.

Law enforcement was the primary institutional approach to the youth gang problem. It emphasized use of single-minded suppression, with little interest in collaborating with other approaches. Youth agencies used referral, treatment, or recreational and, occasionally, outreach youth-worker strategies but without collaboration with law enforcement. Educational organizations emphasized gang prevention, cultural sensitivity, and sometimes special education, but mainly zero tolerance. Neighborhood groups—including home owners, business proprietors, and local citizens—quickly called for police to arrest gang youth. While most politicians and lawmakers denounced gang members and recommended extra punishment for them, some gang experts and social reformers believed that former gang members had to be involved in some positive way in addressing the youth gang problem, and that they were essential to successful gang-control and gang-prevention programs.

Each gang policy and program approach was claimed a success. However, none was adequately articulated and tested with empirical [field-tested, as opposed to theoretical] research. The Little Village Project was different. It was based on the integration of multiple strategies. It was a test of the capacity and willingness of city political, youth-agency, and community leaders to support a comprehensive, collaborative, and balanced approach to the youth gang problem. Closely associated or interrelated with the project was a prospective, quasiexperimental research evaluation to assess its program process, program-youth outcome, and impact on the community gang problem.

Project Formation

In the spring of 1992, just prior to the start of the Little Village Project, a series of changes occurred in city government and selected criminal justice agencies in Chicago, Cook County, and the State of Illinois. A new Chicago mayor was elected, and he appointed a new police superintendent. A former Illinois assistant state's attorney became the director of the Cook County Department of Adult Probation (CCDAP). The then associate director (later the director) of the Illinois Criminal Justice Information Authority (ICJIA) contacted me for a concept paper to create a comprehensive approach to address the worsening gang-violence problem in Chicago.

The idea of the Little Village Gang Violence Reduction Project (GVRP) was quickly accepted with the Chicago Police Department (CPD) as the lead agency, in partnership with the Cook County Department of Adult Probation (CCDAP) and the School of Social Service Administration (SSA) of the University of Chicago. Funding would come from the U.S. Department of Justice's Violence in Urban Areas Program. The goal of the pilot project was to reduce gang homicide, aggravated battery, and assault in six beats of the Tenth Chicago Police District, comprising a mainly Mexican American, low-income working-class community. Violent youth in the two major gangs in the area—the Latin Kings (estimated membership of 12,000) and the Two Six (estimated membership of 8,000)—would be targeted.

The project called for an interagency, community-based team approach to violent gang youth that emphasized a set of interrelated strategies—community mobilization, including formation of a neighborhood advisory group; social intervention through use of outreach youth workers; provision of social opportunities, particularly jobs, training, and access to school programs; a modified suppression strategy by a small group of tactical officers; and organizational change and the development of policies and administrative arrangements to accommodate the new interrelated strategies.

The Role of the Author

The project was reorganized almost before it began. The commander of the gang-crime unit, a key supporter of the project, resigned, and the patrol division assumed minimal responsibility for the two tactical and two neighborhood-relations officers but not for the project. The Chicago Department of Human Services had initially planned to provide outreach youth workers for the project but did not. With experience as a gang worker and administrator of gang projects, I became responsible for developing the outreach youth-work component. The CCDAP followed through on its staffing commitment, but little collaboration occurred between the CPD and CCDAP. A police administrator was not appointed, and I, by default, became the . . . coordinator of the project. The CPD was minimally interested in the development of the project. It was preoccupied with planning and implementing the Chicago Alternative Policing System (CAPS), its new community-policing program.

Entering the Field

The project did not begin in an orderly or carefully planned fashion. It had to make progress in addressing the gang problem in Little Village [a neighborhood on Chicago's west side] within a year. I utilized CPD contacts and official crime data as well as outreach youth workers—mainly former leaders of the Latin Kings and Two Six—to determine which gang sections of the two gangs to target.

The youth workers had no trouble contacting members of the various sections of the two gangs. Their members were omnipresent on the streets from early evening until early the following morning. The assistant director and I, together with the youth workers, explained the purpose and structure of the project, emphasizing the objectives of reducing gang violence, getting youth back to school, and referring them for job training and placement. The assistant director and I told the youth workers that police and probation officers would be on the project team, and together they would help protect the gang guys and the local citizens from gang violence.

By the end of the six months, there was preliminary acceptance of the purpose of the project and the role of youth workers, particularly in respect to helping with job opportunities and gaining access again to school and training. Gang youth more freely provided information about gang situations. Communication by youth with other members of the project team, including police, began to occur. Identifying youth for the program was based mainly on the observations of youth workers and gang-violence arrest reports provided by project tactical police. The project police reviewed arrest reports of all Tenth District officers each day, and recommended and confirmed which particular youth should be targeted.

Contact Between Different Groups in the Project

Youth workers responded to project police and probation officers' requests for information about where program youth hung out and the nature of activities of the gang sections, and verified whether a youth was responsible for a particular gang-violent act. Youth workers did not necessarily share information about all forms of crime in which target youth participated. Project police and probation officers were respectful of youth workers and acknowledged the critical importance of their contacts and services. Project police referred target gang youth for help with school problems and job-related placement or training. From the start, relations between the two project tactical officers and the youth workers were remarkably positive. At the invitation of the youth workers, project police met on the street with members of a section of the Two Six, and then with members of a section of the Latin Kings. Project probation officers also quickly developed good relationships with both the tactical officers and youth workers.

The assistant director and I made contacts with local organizations and community groups to support the development of the project. The park department, several Catholic churches, and a protestant community church made gym and meeting-room facilities available to program youth. Contacts were also made with the administrators of the two local Boys and Girls Clubs, the high school, a major Latino community organization, and the three aldermen [elected city officials] who represented sections of the Little Village community. A local community activist at one of the local community organization meetings volunteered to help with the creation of a neighborhood advisory group to assist the project in its mission of comprehensively addressing the youth gang problem.

Varied evaluation-research aspects of the project's work developed simultaneously. The CPD liaison lieutenant to the project assisted with access to police data and recommended the development of surveys to measure changes in the community's perception of the gang problem. Interviews of program youth began. Arrangements were made to obtain entire police histories of program and comparison youth. Program records began to be completed by the youth workers, police, probation officers, and later, the neighborhood organizer.

The Outreach Youth Worker

The project depended heavily on youth-worker outreach contacts and relationships with gang youth. Most of the outreach youth workers from the community had been former leaders or influential members in the particular gangs to which they were assigned. Use of outreach youth workers made for rapid entry into the gang world and easy targeting of hard-core gang youth by the entire project team. Outreach youth workers were present on the streets of Little Village not only during assigned work hours but at other times as well, since most still lived or had friends and family in the community. They had access to information that served law-enforcement and social-intervention purposes. They engaged gang youth individually or in small groups on the street, at home or in family contexts, on athletic fields, in recreation centers, in detention facilities, at school, on the job, and elsewhere about a range of problems. The youth worker was often involved in a variety of tense field situations.

A primary concern of the youth worker was to help the youth stay out of trouble. He was a proactive communicator and mediator between the target youth and his significant others: family, girlfriend or wife, and representatives of social, educational, employment, and criminal justice agencies. The program gang youth was helped to find a job, complete high school, or pursue further education. However, the traditional role of mediating conflicts between opposing gangs was not generally employed by youth workers. It was easier to encourage lulls in fighting and gain agreement from gang leaders or influentials to "get members to stay in their own neighborhoods." Project team members in general were reluctant to formally mediate conflicts, which would mean recognizing the legitimacy of gang leaders and strengthening their influence in enforcing gang norms and contributing to gang cohesion. The stated view of project staff, including the youth workers, was that gangs were illegitimate structures and that gang life was destructive. Gang youth had to be persuaded or constrained to leave the gang as soon as possible.

Youth Workers and the Rest of the Community

Youth workers assisted local residents and block clubs in addressing problems that contributed to gang delinquency, such as closing down a bar that catered to underage gang youth and permitted the use and sale of narcotics. They were able to support parents and neighbors at times of gang crises, particularly when shootings occurred and gang members (and nongang youth) were injured or killed. The youth workers collaborated with the project police officers in the exchange of information that was vital to the suppression role. On the other hand, the youth workers depended on the project police for information about program youth, as well as for assistance in fulfilling their own roles: protecting them from "hard-nosed" and sometimes brutal police officers in the district who at times harassed and tried to arrest youth workers. The project police often vouched for the youth workers' appropriate presence on the street when they were about to be arrested for gang loitering. (Chicago's gang loitering law was later declared unconstitutional.)

There were problems as well as benefits to the project's use of youth workers who were former members of gangs in the area. When a youth worker's performance problem could not be corrected, I separated the worker from the project but also assisted him in finding another position, enabling him to collect unemployment insurance and maintain health insurance, and assuring that he would remain positively connected to the project. The close interaction of workers in the project team also served as a control mechanism to keep the outreach youth workers conforming to project norms and values. . . .

What Community Groups Should Do to Address the Gang Problem

Those in principal roles must develop a consensus on definitions (e.g., gang, gang incident); specific targets of agency and interagency efforts; and interrelated strategies—based on problem assessment, not assumptions. Coordinated strategies should include the following:

- Community mobilization (including citizens, youth, community groups, and agencies).

- Social and economic opportunities, including special school, training, and job programs. These are especially critical for older gang members who are not in school but may be ready to leave the gang or decrease participation in criminal gang activity for many reasons, including maturation and the need to provide for family.

- Social intervention (especially youth outreach and work with street gangs directed toward mainstreaming youth).

Office of Juvenile Justice and Delinquency Prevention,
March 1999.

Community Mobilization

The priority objectives at the start of the project were the creation of a street-level team to control gang violence and to provide services to targeted youth. These objectives became a basis for organizing an advisory group to the project, which became a quasi-independent neighborhood organization concerned with the gang problem. The CPD was interested in organizing or using a neighborhood group but not a broad group of key community leaders and agency personnel for a community-wide steering committee to advise and direct the development of the project.

The assistant director and I spent a great deal of time, initially, contacting local agencies, churches, colleges, unions, and business groups to develop access to education, training, and jobs for program youth. Special interest and concern about the youth gang problem were expressed by several Catholic churches and a local protestant community church; several Boys and Girls Clubs, the local high school, a job agency, and one of the three aldermen in the wards representing the community were also interested.

A local community activist, with a background as a local alternative-education worker and community organizer, offered to bring agencies, local organizations, and residents together to form an association to support the project. By early spring of 1993, the community activist and the pastor of a local protestant community church had developed a small advisory group. Several community meetings were held, and local citizens expressed concerns about the gang problem. The Catholic churches, two Boys and Girls Clubs, a job agency recruiting workers for factories in the suburbs, one of the local aldermen, and several residents became board members of Neighbors Against Gang Violence (NAGV). Application for a state charter as a nonprofit organization was made and awarded. Funding applications also went to local and national foundations and a state agency.

Neighbors Against Gang Violence

NAGV stated that its goal was "to reduce gang violence in the Little Village Community." Its objectives included establishing four chapters in high-gang-violence areas, recruiting two hundred members, initiating activities to bring the community together, and placing twenty hard-core gang members on jobs or in training. Funding was received from a state agency and a local community foundation. However, there was little effort in organizing residents, businesses, and local agencies by the two NAGV organizers. Several community-wide meetings were held, but attendance was sparse. A good deal of time was spent participating in and organizing recreational activities for GVRP program youth. However, a large and successful community memorial service and mass meeting was held to honor youth victims of gang violence. The interest of NAGV focused more and more on placing youth in jobs and conducting group meetings for parents, some of whose children were not GVRP targeted program youth.

A series of crises occurred in mid-1995 that had long-term effects on the development of NAGV. A gang graffiti paint-out was conducted with one of the project gangs but without contact or involvement of GVRP staff. A youth was shot and killed, and the mother of the victim sued NAGV. Tensions increased between the NAGV board, the community organizer, and project youth-worker staff. Project police officers were also upset that the NAGV organizer charged them with false arrest of a neighborhood youth. Conflict developed between the organizer and the NAGV board. She was accused of "double dipping," obtaining funds from the GVRP and a state grant for the same effort. Community cross-agency meetings were infrequently held. The NAGV organizer became increasingly interested in direct service to youth and less in assisting the project with mobilizing and coordinating community and agency interests in addressing the gang problem. NAGV and GVRP efforts, separately and together, were insufficient to develop an effective neighborhood advisory group for the project and mobilize agency and community interest in the youth gang problem. . . .

Changes in Social Context of Program Youth

There were 195 youth from the two gangs—Latin Kings and Two Six—in the program sample, of whom 127 were interviewed three times in annual periods during the course of the five-year program to ascertain their perceptions of change in community institutions, agency programs, gang membership status, gang structure, peer relationships, family life, employment, educational experience, personal and household income, and future job and income aspirations and expectations. Program youth indicated many changes. They came to view the Little Village community as a better place to live. They were less concerned about family victimization from gang crime. Individual and household income increased slightly more for the Two Six than the Latin Kings. Illegal income was a smaller proportion of individual and household income than legal income but was a larger proportion of total income for Latin Kings and their households. Relationships with mothers, fathers, and siblings continued to be generally positive. The quality of relationships between gang youth and their wives or steady girlfriends was only moderately positive at the time I interview and deteriorated by the time III interview. There was some increase in household health and mental-health crises.

Aging out of the gangs seemed to be correlated with perceived changes in community and personal factors. Toward the end of the program period, many youth in the program declared they were no longer active members of the gang. The drop was particularly marked for the Latin Kings. Educational levels and employment increased for members of both gangs. Latin Kings school dropouts decreased from 52.3 percent to 35.4 percent, and Two Six dropouts decreased from 43.6 percent to 25.8 percent. Latin Kings employment increased from 35.7 percent to 48.2 percent; Two Six employment jumped from 30.9 percent to 63.3 percent. While occupational aspirations fell and occupational expectations rose, income aspirations and expectations remained relatively high for members of both gangs.

Self-Reported Offense Changes in Relation to Life-Course Changes

Program youth were asked whether and how many times they had committed any of sixteen offenses typical of gang members in Little Village. Focus was on serious offenses, especially violence. The analysis was not statistically controlled for pre-program criminal record or length of time in the program, as it was in later ... analyses using arrest data. We found extensive, if not extraordinary, reductions in self-reported offenses and self-reported arrests by almost all program youth between the time I and time III interviews. Most of the reductions were highly statistically significant. There were reductions in serious violence offenses from a mean of 15.5 to 3.6 per youth, and a reduction in drug-selling offenses from a mean of 4.1 to 2.8 per week per youth (but this reduction was not statistically significant). There were also declines in offenses when the units of analysis were the gang (Latin Kings or Two Six), cohort (I, II, or III, that is, entry points of youth into the program), and age group (nineteen and older, seventeen and eighteen, sixteen and younger). The oldest group, nineteen and older, already had the lowest mean level of self-reported offenses at the time I interviews. The seventeen- and eighteen-year-olds self-reported the highest level but also the greatest reduction of offenses at the time III interviews.

Interpreting the Data

We wondered whether there was a correlation between the reduction in self-reported offenses and arrests and changes in life-course and life-space factors. One surprising correlation was the youth's relationships with wives or steady girlfriends and their self-reported offenses. Surprisingly, a poorer or more conflicting relationship with a wife or steady girlfriend between the time I and time III interviews was correlated significantly with a reduction in self-reported total offenses, violence offenses, and property offenses at the time III interview.

Unlike the youth's relationships with mothers, fathers, and siblings, problematic or conflict relationships with wives or steady girlfriends tended to result in reduced levels of offending over time. This could be explained by pressures from wives or steady girlfriends for the program youth to reduce their levels of involvement with the gang. Also, an increase in the amount of time spent with wives and steady girlfriends at the time I or time III interviews was significantly correlated with a reduction in self-reported total offenses, violence offense, and serious violence offenses at the time III interviews.

Certain life-course and life-space factors seemed to be good predictors of reductions of different types of self-reported offenses. The variables ... that [best] predicted reduced total offenses included the youth's contact with a probation officer, more rather than less time spent with a wife or steady girlfriend, and being nineteen years or older. The variables in the best model predicting reduced violence offenses were the youth's satisfaction with the community, his avoidance of gang situations, and more rather than less involvement in treatment for personal problems. The variables in the best model predicting reduced drug-selling activity were more rather than fewer relatives in jail, having a wife or steady girlfriend, and spending more rather than less time on a job.

> *"The fact remains that most of the re-*
> *sources currently committed to the pre-*
> *vention and control of youth violence,*
> *drug use and delinquency, at both na-*
> *tional and local levels, has been in-*
> *vested in unproven programs based on*
> *questionable assumptions and delivered*
> *with little consistency or quality con-*
> *trol."*

Many Gang Prevention Programs Have Not Been Proven Effective

Delbert S. Elliot

In the following viewpoint, Delbert S. Elliot calls for more evaluation of, and higher standards for, youth violence prevention programs in the United States. He argues that it is unclear whether many of the youth violence prevention programs in this country are effective or not, because they have not been evaluated. He suggests that funding for violence prevention needs to be given to programs that have undergone rigorous evaluation and can be implemented systematically. Delbert S. Elliot is the

Delbert S. Elliot, "Preventing Youth and Gang Violence," Testimony of Delbert S. Elliot before the Subcommittee on Crime, Terrorism, and Homeland Security Membership, February 15, 2007. Reproduced by permission of the author.

director of the Center for the Study and Prevention of Violence at the University of Colorado.

As you read, consider the following questions:

1. What percentage of drug and violence prevention/ intervention programs are rigorously evaluated, according to the Center for the Study and Prevention of Violence?

2. According to this viewpoint, what are some of the dangers of programs that have not been evaluated?

3. What would be the cost of putting Life Skills Training in every middle school in the United States, according to this viewpoint?

The demand for effective violence, drug, and crime prevention programs continues to grow. It is now common for Federal and State Agencies, private foundations and other funders to require or at least encourage the use of "evidence-based" programs. While this is an important new direction for current policy, the great majority of programs implemented in our schools and communities still have no credible research evidence for their effectiveness. In their national review of delinquency, drug and violence prevention/intervention programs, the Center for the Study and Prevention of Violence has identified over 600 programs that claim to prevent or deter violence, drug use or delinquent behavior and less than 20% have any rigorous evaluation. There are several reasons for this. First, the new evidence-based policy is typically only a guideline and is not mandated or enforced. The process for selecting programs remains largely informal, relying on local expertise and "old boy/girl networks," and in many instances does not include scientific evidence of effectiveness as an important selection criterion. There is still a relatively strong aversion to "canned" programs developed outside the local area. Second, many of the lists of approved programs provided by funding agencies either have no scientific standard for selection or a very low standard. The scientific evidence for effectiveness is highly questionable for a significant number of lists. Third, few programs on these lists have the capacity to be delivered with fidelity on a wide scale. According to a recent national survey of school-based prevention programs, most programs being implemented were not evidence-based and even when they were, they were often being delivered with such poor fidelity that there is no reason to believe they could be effective in preventing violence, drug use or delinquency. The fact remains that most of the resources currently committed to the prevention and control of youth violence, drug use and delinquency, at both national and local levels, has been invested in unproven programs based on questionable assumptions and delivered with little consistency or quality control.

Moreover, the vast majority of these untested programs continue to be implemented with no plans for evaluation. This means we will never know which (if any) of them have had some significant deterrent effect; we will learn nothing from our investment in these programs to improve our understanding of the causes of violence or to guide our future efforts to deter violence; and there is no meaningful accountability of the expenditures of scarce community resources. Worse yet, some of the most popular programs have actually been demonstrated in careful scientific studies to be ineffective or even harmful, and yet we continue to invest huge sums of money in them for largely political reasons.

The Reasons for Not Evaluating Programs

What accounts for this limited investment in the evaluation of our prevention programs? First, there is little political or program support for evaluation. Federal and state violence prevention initiatives often fail to provide any realistic funding for evaluation of the programs being implemented. Moreover, program directors argue that in the face of limited funding,

Defining "Evidence-Based"

In the health care field, evidence-based practice (or practices), also called EBP or EBPs, generally refers to approaches to prevention or treatment that are validated by some form of documented scientific evidence. What counts as "evidence" varies. Evidence often is defined as findings established through scientific research, such as controlled clinical studies, but other methods of establishing evidence are considered valid as well. Evidence-based practice stands in contrast to approaches that are based on tradition, convention, belief, or anecdotal evidence.

One concern is that too much emphasis on EBPs may in some cases restrict practitioners from exercising their own judgment to provide the best care for individuals. For this reason many organizations have adopted definitions of evidence-based practice that emphasize balancing the "scientific" with the "practical."

National Registry of Evidence-Based
Programs and Practices. www.nrepp.samhsa.gov.

every dollar available should go to the delivery of program services, i.e., to helping youth avoid involvement in violent or criminal behavior. The cost of conducting a rigorous outcome evaluation is prohibitive for most local programs, exceeding their entire annual operational budget in many cases. Without independent funding, they can not undertake a meaningful evaluation. Finally, many program developers believe they know intuitively that their programs work, and thus they do not think a rigorous evaluation is required to demonstrate this.

Negative and Positive Outcomes of Evaluated Programs

Unfortunately, this view is very shortsighted. When rigorous evaluations have been conducted, they often reveal that such programs are ineffective and can even be harmful. Indeed, many programs fail to address any of the known risk factors or underlying causes of violence. Rather, they involve simplistic "silver bullet" assumptions and allocate investments of time and resources that are far too small to counter the years of exposure to negative influences of the family, neighborhood, peer group, and the media. Violence, substance abuse and delinquency involve complex behavior patterns that involve both individual dispositions and social contexts in which these behaviors may be normative and rewarded. There is a tendency for programs to focus only on individual dispositions, with little or no attention to the reinforcements for criminal behavior in the social contexts where youth live. As a result, any positive changes in the individual's behavior achieved in the treatment setting are quickly lost when the youth returns home to his or her family, neighborhood, and old friends. This failure to attend to the social context also accounts for the "deviance training" effect often resulting from putting at-risk youth into correctional settings or other "group" treatment settings which rely on individual treatment models and fail to properly consider the likelihood of emerging delinquent group norms and positive reinforcements for delinquent behavior.

On the positive side, we have a number of very effective violence prevention and intervention programs. We have a universal drug prevention program (Life Skills Training) that can reduce the onset of illicit drugs by 50–70 percent and alcohol and tobacco use by as much as 50 percent; an intervention program for adjudicated youth [those in the juvenile justice system] (Mutisystemic Therapy) that reduces the probability of recidivism [return to criminal behavior] by as much as 75 percent; an early childhood program (Nurse Family Partnership) that reduces arrests by 59 percent. We have the means to significantly reduce current levels of violence and substance abuse, but we are not implementing effective programs on a level that can have any significant effect on overall rates of violence and substance abuse in our communities.

Include Evaluation When Funding Unproven Programs

Progress in our ability to effectively prevent and control crime requires evaluation to identify effective programs and a commitment to implement these programs with fidelity. Only those programs with demonstrated effectiveness and the capacity to be delivered with fidelity should be implemented on a wide scale. We have a long history of pushing untested programs for political reasons only to discover later that they did not work (e.g., DARE [Drug Abuse Resistance Education], boot camps, shock probation, juvenile court transfers/waivers). A responsible accounting to the taxpayers, private foundations, or businesses funding these programs requires that we justify these expenditures with tangible results. No respectable business would invest millions of dollars in an enterprise without assessing its profit potential. No reputable physician would subject a patient to a medical treatment for which there was no evidence of its effectiveness (i.e., no clinical trials to establish its potential positive and negative effects). No program designer should be willing to deliver a program with no effort to determine if it is effective. Our continued failure to provide this type of evidence for prevention programs will seriously undermine public confidence in crime prevention efforts generally. It is at least partly responsible for the current public support for building more prisons and incapacitating youth—the public knows they are receiving some protection for this expenditure, even if it is temporary.

The costs of a randomized control trial is quite high, well beyond the capacity of most programs. Federal funding for promising prevention/intervention programs is critical to advancing both the number of programs that can be certified as effective and the diversity of populations and conditions under which these programs work.

Stop Funding Programs That Don't Work

The available evidence indicates that a number of very popular crime prevention programs don't work and a few appear to be harmful. Some of the better known programs and strategies that appear not to work include: shock probation (e.g., Scared Straight), waivers of juveniles into the adult criminal court, traditional DARE, gun buyback programs, vocational programs, juvenile intensive parole supervision, reduced probation/parole caseloads, and STARS [Start Taking Alcohol Risks Seriously]. Whether the accumulated evidence for these programs is conclusive depends on the standard we use to certify programs as effective or not effective, but there is clearly reason to be very cautious about continuing these programs until some positive evaluation outcomes are obtained.

Clarify "Evidence-Based"

There is a lot of confusion about what constitutes an evidence-based program. There are those who think that positive testimonials by clients is sufficient evidence to claim their program is evidence-based; to be certified as a model program in the Blueprints for Violence Prevention series, the program has to have two random control trials [RCT] or very rigorous quasi-experimental trials that show positive effects plus evidence that the effect is sustained for at least one year after leaving the program. Most of the "lists" of Federal agencies require at least one RCT or quasi-experimental study. This is not a very demanding standard—one study, typically by the designer of the program in a specific location under ideal conditions. The standard for certifying a program as a model program, that is, a program that qualifies to be implemented on a statewide or national level, must have a very high probability of success. Should they fail, we will quickly lose public support for funding them, not only for the program that failed, but for other programs that might be truly effective.

Unfortunately, our record for the success of programs that have been widely implemented (e.g., DARE) has not been very good and that is because we have not required a high scientific standard for programs being implemented on this scale. There is a proposed standard that should be carefully considered. The Working Group of the Federal Collaboration on What Works was established in 2003 to explore how Federal agencies could advance evidence-based crime and substance abuse policy. The Working Group included officials from Department of Justice, Department of Health and Human Services, Department of Education and representatives from the Coalition for Evidence-Based Policy and the National Governor's Association. The Working Group has recommended an excellent standard and classification system for certifying a program's level of demonstrated effectiveness. If this standard was formally adopted, it would both clarify what "evidence-based" means and set a required scientific standard for programs that are considered ready for widespread dissemination.

Promote Cost Effective Evidence-Based Programs

The implementation of evidence-based prevention and intervention programs will result in saved lives, more productive citizens, and significant reductions in crime and violence. The estimated cost for putting Life Skills Training in every middle school in America has been estimated to be $550M[million] per year. This represents less than 2 percent of national spending on drug control ($40B[billion]). The benefits of this program extended beyond the actual participants in the program to their associates and to a shrinking of the drug market allowing for more targeted and effective law enforcement. In this analysis, the effects of law enforcement and prevention/intervention were about the same. Clearly we need both. The Washington State Institute for Public Policy estimates that it would cost about $60M a year to implement a portfolio of evidence-based crime and violence prevention/intervention programs. After four years, the savings associated with reductions in crime would equal the cost of the portfolio; in 10 years, the cost benefit would be $180M; and in 20 years, the cost benefit would be close to $400M for the $60M investment in the evidence-based program portfolio.

Nationally, we are investing far more resources in building and maintaining prisons than in primary prevention or intervention programs. We have put more emphasis on reacting to criminal offenders after the fact and investing in prisons to remove these young people from our communities, than on preventing our children from becoming delinquent and violent offenders in the first place and retaining them in our communities as responsible, productive citizens. Of course, if we had no effective prevention strategies or programs, there is no choice. But we do have effective programs and investing in these programs and the development of additional effective programs is effective, both in terms of human resources and taxpayer savings. Prevention and intervention must be part of a balanced approach to crime reduction.

Periodical Bibliography

The following articles have been selected to supplement the diverse views presented in this chapter.

Anthony A. Braga	"The Strategic Prevention of Gun Violence Among Gang-Involved Offenders," *Justice Quarterly*, March 2008.
Jon Feere and Jessica Vaughan	"Taking Back the Streets: ICE and Local Law Enforcement Target Immigrant Gangs," Center for Immigration Studies, September 2008. www.cis.org/ImmigrantGangs.
Tom Hayden	"Turning Point in the Gang Crisis," *The Guardian*, September 12, 2008.
Thomas J. Lemmer et al.	"An Analysis of Police Responses to Gangs in Chicago," *Police Practice & Research*, December 2008.
Joe Lepper	"Research Centre—Positive Approach to Local Identity Will Combat Gang Violence," *Children Now*, October 23, 2008.
Richard Mertens	"In Chicago, Talking Sense to Angry Young Men with Guns," *Christian Science Monitor*, June 17, 2008.
New York Times	"A Job or a Gang?" (editorial), December 29, 2008.
Raul Reyes	"ICE Raids on Gangs Truly Makes U.S. Safer," *USA Today*, October 10, 2008.
Saba Salman	"Capital Plan for Joint Action on Violence," *The Guardian*, February 11, 2009.
Brigid Schulte	"In the War on Gangs, It's One Kid at a Time: Hands-On Program Gives Teens Options," *Washington Post*, March 20, 2008.

OPPOSING
VIEWPOINTS®
SERIES

CHAPTER 4

What Is the Impact of Gangs?

Chapter Preface

Illegal drug distribution, violence in schools, and the economic cost of crime are all commonly understood impacts of gangs. However, another sometimes overlooked impact that gangs have on society is the corruption of law enforcement officials. Criminal activities that gangs may be involved in, such as the drug trade, are highly lucrative and this can create a situation ripe for corruption. In an October 22, 2008 report, Robert Leventhal, the director of anti-corruption programs at the State Department's Bureau of International and Law Enforcement Affairs, explained, "The huge amount of money generated by the global drug trade allows drug lords to corrupt police, customs and other public officials and establish structures and networks that can be used to facilitate other criminal or terrorist activities."

Corruption is sometimes a problem in police departments. Gangs may pay off officers to turn a blind eye to criminal activities such as drug dealing, sometimes officers even help the gangs with their illicit activities. Investigations in Chicago and New York have found police officers entangled in gangs and organized crime. On February 1, 2008, the *Daily News* reported: "A [New York] city detective was charged yesterday with conspiring to sell crack and tipping off members of a violent drug gang in Brooklyn." Chicago has also recently charged some of its police officers with corruption-related offenses. In October 2007, *The United Press International* reported that seven officers were named in corruption charges and the Special Operations section of the Chicago Police Department was disbanded.

Corruption is also a major problem in prisons. Prison guards and prisoners live in close proximity in an isolated environment, and gang members sometimes enlist the help of guards to carry on their criminal activities outside the prison walls. Steve Gills, a former inmate and current prison advocate in New Zealand, told *The Dominion Post*, "attempts to intimidate staff are common ... [though] some Corrections prison officers are worse than some of the inmates. It doesn't matter what occupation we're talking about, anyone can be bent." *The Dominion Post* goes on to point out that while some corrections officers may be susceptible to the temptation of bribery and lucrative criminal activities, other officers help prisoners with their illegal activities because of threats and intimidation.

The ability of gangs to infiltrate police and other law enforcement officials not only increases their strength but also makes them all the more difficult to snuff out. In the following chapters, the authors discuss the various impacts of gangs. As the above-mentioned cases of corruption demonstrate, sometimes the presence of gangs creates a vicious circle in which the impacts of gangs strengthen the gangs.

| "Crime costs Americans \$655 billion a year."

Gangs Have a Large Economic Impact

Fight Crime: Invest in Kids

In the following viewpoint, Fight Crime: Invest in Kids claims that youth involvement in gang-related homicides is on the rise. The organization contends that there are different types of gangs but that most are involved in drug sales and other criminal activities, arguing that this problem has large economic costs not only to the victims of gang-related crimes but to all taxpayers. Fight Crime: Invest in Kids is a nonprofit, anti-crime organization of law enforcement officials.

As you read, consider the following questions:

1. What percent of homicides in Chicago and Los Angeles does this viewpoint attribute to gangs?
2. What are the three different categories of gangs identified by Fight Crime: Invest in Kids?
3. How much does crime cost a family of four each year even if none of them is the victim of a crime, according to this viewpoint?

William Christeson and Sanford Newman, "Caught in the Crossfire: Arresting Gang Violence by Investing in Kids," Fight Crime: Invest in Kids, 2004, pp. 6–9. Reproduced by permission.

Youth-gang related homicides have risen by more than 50 percent according to Professor James Alan Fox, a leading criminologist at Northeastern University [Boston]. Gang homicides have climbed from 692 in 1999 to over 1,100 in 2002, the latest year for which data is available. Gang-related homicides account for approximately half of all homicides in Chicago, the city that had the highest total number of homicides of any city in the country in 2003. Gang-related homicides also account for approximately half of all homicides in Los Angeles, which led the nation in total homicides the year before (2002).

Gangs are also responsible for the lion's share of juvenile delinquency in smaller cities. A study of troubled youth in Rochester, New York showed that gang members accounted for 68 percent of all the violent acts of delinquency among the youths studied in that city. In Denver, a similar study showed that gang members were responsible for 79 percent of the serious violence committed by that city's youths.

The Spread of Gangs

Los Angeles and Chicago have long been infamous for their traditional gangs: the Crips and Bloods in LA [Los Angeles] and the Black Gangster Disciples, Latin Kings and Vice Lords in Chicago. But gangs are spreading rapidly throughout the country. According to criminologist Terence Thornberry, "in the space of about 10 years, gangs have spread from a relatively small number of cities to being a regular feature of the urban landscape." The latest Department of Justice funded National Youth Gang Survey in 2003 confirms that all large cities with populations over 250,000 report having gang activity, as do 87 percent of cities with between 100,000 and 250,000 people. However, gangs are not just in cities: 38 percent of suburban counties and 12 percent of rural counties report gang activity as well.

Former Commander Wayne Wiberg of Chicago's narcotics unit explained that gang members are now appearing in smaller cities and towns throughout Illinois. These towns have "not just people living there who are using drugs, but people living there that are selling."

The Development and Types of Gangs

Youth gangs have been around for a long time. In the early 19th century, youth gangs were primarily Irish, Jewish, and Italian when many members of those immigrant groups lived in economically deprived neighborhoods and endured ethnic or religious discrimination. According to the most recent National Youth Gang Survey, nearly half of all gang members are Hispanic and a third are African American. The most recent gangs forming in smaller cities and suburbs in the 1990s, however, are more likely to be mixed ethnically, and involve female, white, and middle-class youths. Gangs vary tremendously, but it is helpful to think in terms of three different categories: traditional gangs; more recent crews, cliques, or posses; and gangs forming in smaller cities, rural areas, and suburbs during the 1990s.

Traditional Gangs

The gangs forming before the mid-1980s tended to fit the traditional definition of gangs. They began defending turf but often evolved into very large organizations that became more involved in drug sales and other criminal activity. Automatic weapons and drive-by shootings replaced the fists, chains and knives used in earlier gang violence. While the average size of traditional gangs is about 180 members, a few of these gangs number in the thousand and even tens of thousands and have formed very elaborate structures and rules similar in many ways to the Mafia. Some gangs, such as the Crips and the Bloods from Los Angeles attempted to set up chapters in other cities. However, most expansion of gangs was home-

Homicide Type by Age, 1976–2005

	Victims				Offenders			
	Under 18	18–34	35–49	50+	Under 18	18–34	35–49	50+
All homicides	9.8%	52.7%	22.8%	14.7%	10.9%	65.0%	17.3%	6.8%
Victim/offender relationship								
Intimate	1.5%	46.7%	34.3%	17.5%	1.0%	46.2%	34.9%	17.9%
Family	19.6%	31.9%	26.4%	22.1%	6.0%	49.1%	28.1%	16.8%
Infanticide	100.0%				7.9%	81.3%	9.7%	1.1%
Eldercide				100.0%	10.3%	49.2%	19.1%	21.4%
Circumstances								
Felony murder	7.6%	46.9%	21.8%	23.8%	14.8%	72.9%	10.3%	2.0%
Sex related	19.6%	45.1%	16.6%	18.7%	10.7%	73.6%	13.7%	2.0%
Drug related	5.4%	71.4%	19.9%	3.3%	10.6%	76.9%	11.3%	1.2%
Gang related	24.2%	68.4%	6.1%	1.3%	28.9%	69.2%	1.6%	.3%
Argument	5.5%	56.1%	26.3%	12.2%	6.9%	60.2%	23.1%	9.7%
Workplace	.5%	28.0%	32.0%	39.5%	3.7%	53.1%	27.6%	15.5%
Weapon								
Gun homicide	7.4%	59.3%	22.4%	10.9%	11.9%	64.8%	15.8%	7.5%
Arson	28.3%	27.0%	19.2%	25.5%	11.5%	57.7%	23.8%	7.0%
Poison	28.0%	23.3%	16.5%	32.2%	4.5%	50.9%	26.2%	18.5%
Multiple victims or offenders								
Multiple victims	18.2%	46.3%	19.1%	16.4%	9.5%	66.1%	18.5%	5.9%
Multiple offenders	11.3%	55.5%	19.7%	13.5%	18.2%	73.1%	7.5%	1.2%

TAKEN FROM: FBI, *Supplementary Homicide Reports, 1976–2005.*

grown or due to members simply moving to other cities, rather than a more concerted franchising effort.

More Recent Crews, Cliques, or Posses

Many cities, like Washington D.C. and Philadelphia, have relatively few of the larger, more traditional gangs, and instead have more loosely structured neighborhood "crews", "cliques", or "posses". These small drug or neighborhood gangs often number only 25 members, and there is less gang graffiti, hand signs, and "colors" associated with these groups. Still "Live by the neighborhood, die by the neighborhood" is a common sentiment for these smaller gangs. These neighborhood gangs that often formed during the early 1980s are the most likely of any of the three categories of gangs to be involved in drug sales.

Gangs Forming in Smaller Cities, Rural Areas, and the Suburbs During the 1990s

Compared to the more traditional gangs and the crews, cliques, or posses that formed in the 1980s, the newer gangs forming in smaller cities, rural areas, and the suburbs beginning in the 1990s tend to be less involved in both drug sales and violence. As mentioned above, these newer gangs are often more diverse, and more likely to have white, female, and even middle-class members. Some of these gangs are small collections of youths that take on ominous names similar to traditional gangs and are involved in graffiti, etc., but may not be especially violent or heavily involved in drug sales. Nevertheless the difference between some of these newer gangs and other earlier gangs may not be that great, and parents, the police, and communities need to be vigilant. These newer gangs may become more dangerous over time. There are also very violent inner-city drug gangs or more traditional-style gangs, such as the El Salvadoran dominated MS-13, whose members are moving into the older, close-in suburbs near many cities.

Gangs, Crime Trends, and Costs

From a peak in the early 1990s, violent crime and homicide rates have dropped dramatically. But there is no room for Americans to become complacent. Violent crime in America is still at unacceptable levels: in 2001 over 16,000 Americans lost their lives to violence. And in 2002, homicides were up over two percent and then again another one percent for the first six months of 2003 (the latest available national figures). When crime last began to spike upwards in the late 1980s and early 1990s cities with more than one million people were the first cities to see crime go up and then the first to see it come down. So it is alarming that homicides were heading up almost six percent in those largest cities for the first six months of 2003. And certainly the sharp increase in youth-gang related homicides is a related and especially ominous trend.

Crime costs Americans $655 billion a year. Most of that cost is borne by the millions of victims, but Americans also pay $90 billion a year in taxes for criminal justice system expenses and an additional $65 billion a year in total private security costs. The taxes and private security payments alone average $535 dollars a year for every man, woman and child in America. That is over $2,000 for a family of four even if no one in that family becomes a victim of the more than 23 million crimes committed each year in the United States. In a 1998 study, Professor Mark A. Cohen of Vanderbilt University [Nashville, Tennessee] looked at the cost issue from another perspective. He found that preventing one teen from adopting a life of crime would save the country between $1.7 million and $2.3 million. The Department of Justice reports that "if the 2001 rates of incarceration were to continue indefinitely" a white male in the United States would have a 1 in 17 chance of going to state or federal prison during his lifetime, a Hispanic male would have a 1 in 6 chance and a black male would have a 1 in 3 chance of going to prison. However one looks at it—the more than 16,000 homicides a year, the millions of young men and women who will be imprisoned, or the shattered lives of the survivors of crime—crime and violence continue to challenge the very soul of America.

Real Hope for Reducing the Toll of Gang Violence

After years of contentious debate about whether to be tougher or more compassionate with criminals, a consensus is beginning to emerge in some communities. The consensus is based on a combination of research, hard experience gained from those in closest contact with these troubled youths, and a willingness by policy-makers to leave ideological suppositions behind to adopt tested, proven solutions. Law enforcement leaders are often leading this change. The real solutions are to be found in becoming smarter about crime, which requires new policies that are both tough and compassionate. If the right policies are followed, the huge costs and the lives lost because of violent crime can be sharply reduced.

> *"The [National Drug Intelligence Center] affirms that gangs involved in drug crimes are responsible for violent 'assaults, carjackings, drive-by shootings, home invasions, robberies and firearms violations."*

Gangs Often Traffic in Drugs

Nicholas V. Lampson

In the following viewpoint, Nicholas V. Lampson introduces a bill that would heavily penalize criminals involved in drug trafficking. Lampson blames increased gang activity in the Houston, Texas, area for increased drug trafficking. Nicholas V. Lampson is the United States Representative from the 22nd District in Texas.

As you read, consider the following questions:

1. What does the author believe to be the reason for the increase in crime in Houston from 2005 to 2006?

2. Why, according to the author, do gangs commit crimes such as assaults and carjackings?

3. Why, according to the National Center for Missing and Exploited Children, do many young people join gangs?

Nicholas V. Lampson, "Gang Crime Prevention," Capitol Hill Hearing Testimony, *Congressional Quarterly*, October 2, 2007. Reproduced by permission.

Thank you for taking my testimony today about my efforts to catch, prosecute and incarcerate gang members.

Gang participation has reached unacceptable levels in our country and is threatening the safety and security of big cities, as well as small towns. According [to the] Department of Justice [DOJ], 82% of police departments serving large cities have reported youth gangs while the DOJ also reports gang activity has been increasing in smaller cities since 1999.

Gang Drug Trafficking in Houston

In my district, in Houston [Texas], crime has been on the rise, FBI [Federal Bureau of Investigation] reports growing trends of murder, rape and assault from 2005 to 2006. According to law enforcement officials, much of this increase in crime in Houston is related to the relocation of street gangs and drug traffickers from New Orleans following Hurricane Katrina. The New Orleans gangs are extremely violent and intimidate many of the established Houston gangs. As such, gang-related crime, particularly gang-related murders, has increased significantly. Additionally, New Orleans gangs have expressed intent to take over large portions of the Houston drug market, which could lead to further violence.

We must be vigilant to protect our communities from these thugs and criminals. Recently I introduced the Prosecutorial Tools Improvement Act of 2007, which will make our homes safer by providing greater latitude and resources to our nation's prosecutors to go after gangs with the fullest extent of the law.

H.R. [House of Representatives bill] 3462 protects families and communities by enhancing criminal penalties for violent felonies committed during and in relation to drug trafficking crimes. According to the National Drug Intelligence Center (NDIC), high levels of violent crime in Houston, Texas are "closely associated with the distribution and abuse of illicit

The Relationship Between Drugs and Gangs

Street gang members convert powdered cocaine into crack cocaine and produce most of the PCP [phencyclidine, another street drug] available in the United States. Gangs, primarily OMGs [outlaw motorcycle gangs], also produce marijuana and methamphetamine. In addition, gangs increasingly are involved in smuggling large quantities of cocaine and marijuana and lesser quantities of heroin, methamphetamine, and MDMA (also known as ecstasy) into the United States from foreign sources of supply. Gangs primarily transport and distribute powdered cocaine, crack cocaine, heroin, marijuana, methamphetamine, MDMA, and PCP in the United States.

Located throughout the country, street gangs vary in size, composition, and structure. Large, nationally affiliated street gangs pose the greatest threat because they smuggle, produce, transport, and distribute large quantities of illicit drugs throughout the country and are extremely violent. Local street gangs in rural, suburban, and urban areas pose a low but growing threat. Local street gangs transport and distribute drugs within very specific areas.

National Drug Intelligence Center,
U.S. Department of Justice.

drugs, particularly crack cocaine and methamphetamine. Crack cocaine is the drug most associated with violent and property crime."

The NDIC affirms that gangs involved in drug crimes are responsible for violent "assaults, carjackings, drive-by shootings, home invasions, robberies, and firearms violations." They commit these acts "to protect and expand their drug operations." These criminal activities must be stopped. My legislation sends a strong and clear message—we will catch you, and we will put you in jail.

Texas' highways have become thoroughfares for the drug trade, unfortunately Houston has become the on ramp. The Texas Highway Patrol leads the nation in criminal arrests and seizures of drugs and currency, between 60 and 80 percent of drugs pass through Houston alone.

A Proposed Solution

My bill imposes stiff penalties for crimes committed by drug traffickers and gangs that participate in drug trafficking. The Prosecutorial Tools Improvement Act of 2007 mandates a life sentence for incidents of murder or kidnapping that are in relation to drug trafficking. Other violent felonies will result in imprisonment for a minimum of 30 years. And crimes such as, conspiracy to commit a violent crime, will result in imprisonment for a minimum of 10 to 20 years.

By instituting harsher penalties, and strengthening the consequences for gang involvement, prosecutors will be given tools they need to pursue and punish modern gangs.

According to the National Center for Missing and Exploited Children, NCMEC, the income drug trafficking provides for gangs serves to attract many young people, especially runaways and homeless children.

NCMEC has outlined that gang activity, when combined with the trafficking of crack or other drugs is "becoming increasingly involved in the prostitution of youth," which can prove to be very profitable for gangs.

As co-chairman and founder of the Congressional Missing and Exploited Children Caucus, this is an issue of the utmost importance to me. As a father and grandfather, I know that the protection of our children is paramount. We can deter our nation's children from joining gangs, by imposing stiff penalties for gang activity, as well as providing opportunities for young people in their community that keeps them off the street.

Finally, my bill increases the ability for our law enforcement agencies to pursue terrorists by increasing the statute of limitations from eight years to ten. Terrorism is the greatest threat we face as a free nation, time should not stand between terrorists and justice. We must ensure that prosecutors have every tool they need to fight terrorism.

Gangs cause irreparable damage to communities and families throughout the United States. My bill gives prosecutors the tools they need to stop gang violence from invading our neighborhoods. Violent Gang complaints are up 38 percent since 2002, but convictions have only increased 12 percent. Clearly, we need more tools and resources to combat and stop gangs. That is exactly what my bill, the Prosecutorial Tools Improvement Act, does.

> "However, in relation to most other drug types, [gang members] were either no more likely or less likely to have used them."

Not All Gang Members Are Involved in Drugs

Trevor Bennett and Katy Holloway

In the following viewpoint, the authors analyse various types and stereotypes of gangs. They discuss the relationship between criminal behavior and gang membership in the United Kingdom, and past research on gangs and criminality in the United States. Finally, they give evidence to support their argument that gang members, at least in their study, are not more likely to use drugs than youths who are not members of a gang. Trevor Bennett and Katy Holloway are both professors at the University of Glamorgan in Pontypridd, Wales.

As you read, consider the following questions:

1. What proportion of the gang members studied had stolen a car within the last 12 months?

2. According to this article, what percentage of reported criminal offenses are gang members responsible for?

3. According to this article, what is the only drug that gang members were more likely than nonmembers to have used in the last 12 months?

There is growing debate in the United Kingdom on the number and nature of street gangs and their contribution to crime and violence. However, the discussion is impeded to some extent by a lack of agreement on the definition of what constitutes a gang. Confusion over definitions of gangs is not confined to the United Kingdom. [Researcher Malcolm] Klein argued that the concept of gangs in the United States has been shaped by the stereotype of the *West Side Story* gang [the 1960s musical was about gang rivalry in New York] and the image of gang 'colors'. He argued that both are distortions of reality, and that few American gangs fit this stereotype. He argues instead that gang formations are much more variable and proposes a typology of observable gang structures based on five discrete forms (traditional, neo-traditional, compressed, collective, and specialty). [Researcher Scott H.] Decker argued that the concept of the gang has been distorted by the dominance of the view that gangs are well organized and tightly structured. However, an alternative view, supported by his own research, shows that gangs are often disorganized and typically do not have leaders.

It is not necessary to enter into the complexities of this debate in this chapter [of *Drug-Crime Connections*] because it has been discussed at length elsewhere. However, it is worth noting that the aim of this chapter is to investigate what are typically called 'street gangs' or 'youth gangs' rather than 'criminal gangs' or 'crime firms' that come together solely to commit a particular criminal act and then disperse. Street gangs are defined by Klein as groups based on a strong gang identity, moderate levels of organization, versatile offending patterns (with some exceptions), amplification of criminal behavior over time, and a variety of structures.

Given the level of current interest in the development of street gangs in the United Kingdom, it is perhaps surprising that so little attention has been paid by British criminologists to the subject. This has resulted in important gaps in our knowledge about the number and distribution of gangs and basic facts about the characteristics of gang members. There are also important gaps in what is known about the contribution of street gangs to criminal behavior, including the extent of gun possession, involvement in violence, drug dealing, drug misuse, and criminal behavior. However, there is some research on gangs that provides information on the characteristics and criminal behavior of gang members. . . .

Problem Behaviors and Gang Membership

Gang members are of particular interest to criminologists because they are commonly involved in various kinds of illegal or deviant behavior. In particular, gang research shows that gang members often commit violent crimes (including homicide), carry guns, commit a broad spectrum of offense types, supply drugs, consume drugs, commit criminal damage (including gang graffiti), and engage in general disorder (some of which leads to fear of gangs among residents).

The NEW-ADAM [New English and Welsh Arrestee Drug Abuse Monitoring] program collected a wide range of information on the criminal behavior of arrestees, and it is possible to test some of the assumptions mentioned using the sample of UK gang members.

Gang members (current and past) were more likely than non–gang members to report committing one or more of [seven possible] property crimes . . . in the last 12 months. However, current gang members were different from non–gang members only in relation to the offenses of theft of a vehicle and handling stolen goods. Over one-fifth of gang members said that they had stolen a vehicle in the last 12 months, and almost half (45%) said that they had handled stolen

177

Gangs and Drug Use

Gang members do not all use drugs or do not use them extensively. Studies also show differences in the extent of drug use. For example, [researchers Karl G.] Hill, [James C] Howell, and [J.] Hawkins found that gang membership was related to increased marijuana use but not crack cocaine use (except among youth who were in the gang for only 1 year). [Researcher Ronald C.] Huff reported gangs that used large amounts of all kinds of drugs. [Researcher J.] Fagan found variations in drug use among different gangs and several other studies found predominantly drug-trafficking youth gangs.

For the most part, the findings of the studies outlined in the previous paragraph apply only to males. Some cities, such as Detroit and San Francisco, found an increasing number of females involved in gang drug trafficking and violent crime, but the consensus is that female involvement in these behaviors has not increased commensurately with the increase among males.

Office of Juvenile Justice and Delinquency Prevention,
Juvenile Justice Bulletin, January 1999.

goods. The connection with youth gangs and vehicle theft is consistent with ethnographic research in the United States, which shows the importance of vehicles in the 'street culture' of gangs. [Researchers Bruce A.] Jacobs, [V.] Topalli, and [R.] Wright found that carjackers interviewed in St. Louis, Missouri, said that they sometimes used cars for joyriding and for showing off to their friends. Decker and [Barrik] van Winkle reported that cruising in cars was a common pursuit among gang members and cited car theft as one of the most common crimes committed by gang members.

Gang members were significantly more likely than non–gang members to have committed robbery. The highest robbery rates were among current gang members. Again, the link with robbery and gang membership is consistent with the US research. There was no connection with gang membership and theft from a person. Gang members were also much more likely than non–gang members to be involved in drug supply offenses. Almost one-third (30%) of current gang members said that they had committed drug supply offenses in the last 12 months.

Comparison with US Research

The North American research literature suggests that gang members are typically involved in a wide range of criminal behavior. This generalist approach to crime has sometimes been referred to as 'cafeteria style' offending. The current findings show that gang members were more likely than non–gang members to be generalists in terms of offending with over a fifth of current gang members and just under a quarter of past gang members reporting committing three or more of the ten offense types. This compares with just over 10 percent of non–gang members. Gang members (current and past) also committed a greater total number of offenses over the last 12 months. Current gang members committed over five times the number of offenses committed by non–gang members.

US surveys of gang and non–gang members also show that gang members commit a disproportionate share of all offenses. [Sociologist Terence] Thornberry reported that gang members comprised about one-third of all youths sampled in the Rochester Youth Development Study. However, they were responsible for 86 percent of acts of serious delinquency, 68 percent of violent acts, and 70 percent of drug sales. The current research shows that gang members (current and past) comprised 15 percent of the total sample of arrestees. However, they were responsible for 31 percent of all offenses reported. This included 89 percent of all robberies, 49 percent of burglaries in a dwelling, 41 percent of thefts of a motor vehicle, 38 percent of burglaries in nondwellings, 36 percent of drug supply offenses, 35 percent of thefts from a vehicle, 28 percent of handling offenses, 26 percent of frauds, and 21 percent of shoplifting offenses.

Gang members were also more heavily involved in possession of weapons and guns. All comparisons between gang members and non–gang members were highly significant. About two-thirds of current gang members had taken a weapon to commit an offense. Over half had possessed a gun, and three-quarters said that they had mixed with people who possessed guns. One-third of gang members said that they had taken a gun with them when committing an offense and two-thirds of gang members said that they had fired a gun.

Overall, the findings are consistent with the image of street gangs from research in the United States. Gang members tend to be involved in criminal behavior, generalists in terms of offending pattern, responsible for a notable proportion of all offenses, sometimes violent, involved in drug supply offenses, and have a tendency to carry weapons and guns (and sometimes use them).

Gangs and Drugs

The United States research is less clear on the extent to which gang members actually use drugs (as opposed to dealing in drugs). [Researcher William B.] Sanders argued that previous ethnographic research of gangs has produced mixed findings. A number of studies refer to frequent 'partying' among gang members, which typically involves alcohol and drug misuse. There are also a number of studies showing that some gangs do not permit heroin misuse because their members would be considered unreliable in gang fights. Sanders's own study of gang members in San Diego found that there were no negative sanctions against use of heroin but some sanctions against use of crack, especially when the gang member was supposed to be selling it.

The problem of drug use among gang members is also confounded by the fact that gang members are also young people with their own particular combination of risk and protective factors relating to drug misuse. [Researcher J.] Fagan argued that comparisons of gang and non–gang youths from similar social backgrounds are rare. In the absence of such studies, it is difficult to know whether gang members are in any sense different from non–gang members in terms of substance abuse. Fagan's own research aimed specifically at identifying differences in drug use behavior among gang and non–gang members by conducting surveys of school students and school dropouts. He found that gang members had higher prevalence rates and higher incidence rates than non–gang members in relation to 'drug misuse' (a scale based on seven drug types). Gang members were also more likely than non–gang members to be involved in the most serious forms of drug misuse (including use of heroin and cocaine).

Differences Shown by the Current Study

Current gang members were significantly more likely than non–gang members to have used cannabis [marijuana] in the last 12 months. However, in relation to most other drug types, they were either no more likely or less likely to have used them. Current gang members were significantly less likely than non–gang members to have used heroin in the last 12 months. They were also slightly less likely (but not significantly so) to have used crack and cocaine. Current gang members were also significantly less likely than non–gang members to report injecting a drug. There was no significant difference among gang and non–gang members in dependency on drugs or expenditure on drugs in the last seven days.

These results do not suggest that gang members are more involved in drug misuse than non–gang members. In fact, there is some evidence that they are less likely to be involved in certain kinds of drug misuse and less likely to report some of the more major problems associated with drug misuse, including use of the more serious drug types and the use of injection.

> *"Even as school officials struggled . . . to provide a sense of security for children in Cypress Park, a 50-foot patch of grass was all that separated second-grade classrooms at Aragon from the rose- and candle- strewn memorial to Marcos Salas, shot 17 times in a flare of gang violence."*

Gangs Disrupt Schools

Susannah Rosenblatt

In the following viewpoint, Susannah Rosenblatt describes how a gang-related drive-by shooting affected schools in the Glassell Park and Cypress Park neighborhoods of Los Angeles. Schools were locked down for several hours keeping students separated from their parents well past normal school hours. In addition to their grief, the author explains that students, parents and school staff are now living with the fear that one of the gangs involved in the shooting will return for revenge. Susannah Rosenblatt is a staff writer for the Los Angeles Times.

As you read, consider the following questions:

1. Why were several schools locked down in Glassell Park on February 21, 2008?

2. Why on the day of the shooting did students at Aragon Elementary School have to leave through an alternative exit?

3. Why according to one parent of an Aragon student is the violence not going to stop?

Third-grader Monic Santana has stopped playing in the yard at Aragon Avenue Elementary since a man was gunned down late last week [February 21, 2008] at the edge of her school's front lawn.

She's scared, she said. And she has to watch out for her younger brother, Salvador, 7, who said he worries "that they're going to get me and kill me."

Even as school officials struggled Monday [February 25, 2008] to provide a sense of security for children in Cypress Park [Los Angeles], a 50-foot patch of grass was all that separated second-grade classrooms at Aragon from the rose- and candle-strewn memorial to Marcos Salas, shot 17 times in a flare of gang violence. He later died.

Police arrested a fourth suspect in the killing Monday afternoon in the San Fernando Valley [southern California]. The suspect, whose name was not released, was described as the driver of the car from which the gunshots were fired and a reputed member of the Avenues street gang, which is blamed for the violence.

Schools Respond to the Shooting

Thursday's [February 21, 2008] drive-by was followed quickly by gunfire from pedestrians who apparently knew Salas, 36, and then by a police shootout about 10 blocks away that left an AK-47-toting gang member dead and another suspect

Schools Do Not Have Enough Funding to Fight Violence

[New York Senator Charles] Schumer said that the Administration has repeatedly cut funding for programs meant to provide vital safety and security funding for schools in upstate New York and across the country. From a high of $180 million in 2002, the COPS [Community Oriented Policing Service] in Schools program has been steadily reduced until funding was completely eliminated for . . . 2006, and it is zeroed out in this year's budget.

"When the federal government draws back funding, it means our schools have to take money away from other vital programs that we all care about. School districts [shouldn't] have to rob Peter to pay Paul in order to protect our kids."

States News Service,
January 31, 2007.

wounded. In the manhunt that followed in neighboring Glassell Park, dozens of blocks and several schools were shut down, separating parents and children well into the evening. The lockdown, officials said, was the longest and the largest many had dealt with.

"This is very fresh," said Kimberly Noble, principal of Washington Irving Middle School in Glassell Park, of the violence that rocked the surrounding neighborhood Thursday. With nearly 1,500 students trapped inside under police order until after 6 p.m., Noble had to improvise a plan to manage the children and anxious parents, standing in the rain and dark waiting for answers about their youngsters locked inside.

Salina Fogel, 36, a sixth-grade math and science teacher at Irving, distributed two M&Ms each to her famished students during their six-hour stay in a temporary classroom building as they watched the movie "Hoodwinked!" and played Othello to pass the time.

"For 11- and 12-year-olds, to go through that, they were brave," she said.

When parents were finally reunited with sixth-graders in Irving's cafeteria, "you could see the wildness, the scaredness" in the adults' eyes, Fogel said.

School district officials believe principals' response worked well, considering the emergency situation.

"Schools are the safe haven in any neighborhood," said Wayne Moore, Los Angeles Unified School District director for school operations. "All of this ruckus was happening around the school," he said, and yet Aragon was "probably one of the safest places to be."

The Students at Aragon Elementary School

Although Aragon students were able to leave at the usual time, about 2:15 p.m., Principal Louis Carrillo had to usher them out an alternative exit because the regular gates were only steps away from where Salas, holding his 2-year-old granddaughter, was slain.

Monic Santana, 9, heard the gunshots and ran to the Aragon bathroom for cover, terrified. She was soon rounded up by her teacher and ended up watching "Scooby-Doo" in the school auditorium. But she couldn't keep her mind on the movie, she said, fearing "that they killed the little baby."

Playground and cafeteria monitor Juana Arevalo estimated that as many as 40 children were playing outside when Salas was shot less than a block away.

Rosa Gutierrez said her little boy Juan told her he saw the shooting through the chain-link fence.

"He didn't want to talk, he was, like, shocked," said Gutierrez, 34. The second-grader "didn't want to come to school the next day." But his mother took the 8-year-old in anyway to speak to a counselor: "Probably he still needs help," she said.

About 10% of the 630 youngsters at Aragon have been referred to psychologists and other crisis workers, Carrillo, the principal, said. But even with a battery of crisis counselors on hand, the school can't erase skittish parents' fears of what might be next.

How Parents Are Dealing with the Incident

"It's not going to stop," said stay-at-home mother Angie Yerena of the intensifying violence in the neighborhood. Her daughter Camille, 6, is a first-grader at Aragon. The little girl, Yerena says, already knows what to do when she hears gunshots: Duck and roll. "They're going to come back," Yerena said, "One or the other is going to retaliate. We're still not in the safe zone."

Aragon, Irving and Fletcher Drive Elementary in Glassell Park sent letters home to parents . . . , and several school and community meetings are planned . . . to address parents' concerns about school safety and neighborhood violence. Aragon has requested and received additional police presence nearby, and a school police officer has been newly assigned to Irving.

But the teachers remain on edge, said Jane De Haven, a fifth-grade teacher at Aragon.

"We realized how dicey it is," De Haven said, recounting that one teacher found bullets lodged in a classroom window. "It could have been any one of us."

> "After taking into account certain socio-economic and demographic factors, Bessette concluded gangs don't bring violence to school, but do foster feelings of insecurity."

Gangs Do Not Increase Violence in Schools

Sarah Schmidt

In the following viewpoint, Sarah Schmidt summarizes the findings of a study conducted by Catherine Bessette as part of her master's degree. In her study of 65 schools in the province of Quebec, Bessette found that the presence of gangs in schools increased students' fears but did not make them more likely to be the victims of a crime. Sarah Schmidt reports on educational issues for the CanWest News Service, a Canadian news agency.

As you read, consider the following questions:

1. According to the study cited in the article, what percentage of students had witnessed fights at school?

2. According to the study's author, why is the presence of gangs in schools still problematic, even if their presence does not increase crime rates?

3. What kind of data did the study's author gather?

An overwhelming majority of high school students witness fights at school but the presence of organized gangs has no effect on the rate of violent incidents, according to the first Canadian study on schools, gangs and violence.

The study—conducted at 65 high schools in disadvantaged communities throughout Quebec—found street gangs in schools don't influence the acts of violence perpetrated there.

At the same time, Universite de Montreal criminologist Catherine Bessette found violent incidents and feelings of insecurity run rampant in schools.

The Numbers

Eighty-four per cent of students had witnessed fights, while 60 per cent witnessed physical attacks and thefts.

One-third of students (34 per cent) witnessed a peer carrying a weapon inside school, while more than one-quarter (28 per cent) reported they did not feel secure at school.

This number increases to 37 per cent when bus stops and schoolyards are included.

The Researcher's Conclusions

After taking into account certain socio-economic and demographic factors, Bessette concluded gangs don't bring violence to school, but do foster feelings of insecurity.

"The presence of gangs doesn't influence student victimization, but it does bring them insecurity," she said in an interview.

Bessette characterizes this finding as "astonishing."

"Street gangs only have an influence on perception and feeling. This could mean that these groups contribute to students' fear even if it doesn't hurt them directly.

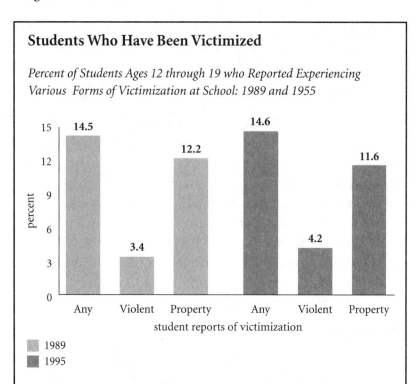

Students Who Have Been Victimized

*Percent of Students Ages 12 through 19 who Reported Experiencing
Various Forms of Victimization at School: 1989 and 1955*

student reports of victimization

■ 1989
■ 1995

TAKEN FROM: U.S. Department of Justice, Bureau of Justice Statistics,
School Crime Supplement to the National Crime Victimization Survey,
spring 1989 and 1995.

"All these results let us conclude that the noxious impact
of gangs in schools is not as severe or direct as we might have
thought," the study concludes.

Still, Bessette said the findings are troubling.

"Violence or not, the feelings of insecurity prompted by
gangs is harmful for youngsters in a learning environment.
The fact that it is constant creates problems for both students
and teachers. This cannot be taken lightly."

Bessette analyzed data collected by the Quebec Department of Education, involving interviews with more than
26,000 students in Grades 7 to 12, to determine the influence
of street gangs on perceived violence, victimization and feeling
of safety in schools.

Wider Implications of the Study

She said there is no reason to believe the climate differs dramatically in schools in disadvantaged neighourhoods across the country.

"We could say that what's going on here in Quebec is going on in the other provinces," Bessette said.

Kathleen Gallagher, academic director of the Centre for Urban Schooling at the Ontario Institute for Studies in Education of the University of Toronto, said this is the first study that appears to control for socio-economic and demographic factors to draw conclusions about gangs and violence in schools.

"I'm intrigued by what the researcher was pulling together," said Gallagher, author of the coming book *The Theatre of Urban: Youth and Schooling in Dangerous Times.*

Periodical Bibliography

The following articles have been selected to supplement the diverse views presented in this chapter.

Dominic Hayes "Death Threats Against Teachers Who Speak Out: Schools Buckling Under the Strain of Battling Gang Culture," *Evening Standard*, February 16, 2007.

James C. Howell "The Impact of Gangs on Communities," *National Youth Gang Center Bulletin*, August 2006. www.iir.com/nygc/publications/ NYGCbulletin_0806.pdf.

Beth M. Huebner "Gangs, Guns, and Drugs: Recidivism Among Serious, Young Offenders," *Criminology & Public Policy*, May 2007.

Sara Miller Llana "New Target for Mexico's Drug Cartels: Schools," *Christian Science Monitor*, December 19, 2008.

Roberto Lovato "The Smog of Race War in LA," *The Nation*, March 21, 2007.

James C. McKinley Jr. "Mexico Hits Drug Gangs with Full Fury of War," *New York Times*, January 22, 2008.

Gareth Morgan "Raiding and Rioting; Exclusive Gang Warfare Is Turning Our Schools into a Battle Zone," *The People* (London), June 8, 2008.

Reynaldo Reyes III "Cholo to 'Me': From Peripherality to Practicing Student Success for a Chicano Former Gang Member," *Urban Review*, June 2006.

Mark Stevenson "Police: Drug Turf Battles near Mexico's Capital," *Associated Press*, February 12, 2009.

Avelardo Valdez "The Drugs-Violence Nexus Among Mexican-American Gang Members," *Journal of Psychoactive Drugs*, June 2006.

For Further Discussion

Chapter 1

1. After reading Eloisa Ruano Gonzalez's and Joan Smith's viewpoints on girls in gangs, how do you think girls' involvement in gangs changes theproblem? Do you think possible solutions to the gang problem need to bere-thought to account for the involvement of girls?

2. In the viewpoint "Gangs Are a Problem of the Underprivileged,"Ely Flores argues that institutions contribute to the social oppression thatleads some people to join gangs. Do you agree with Flores? Why or whynot?

3. The viewpoint by *The Economist* begins by refuting the conventional wisdom that admitting more immigrants to Great Britain leads to higher crime rates. How is the argument refuted? Do you find the rebuttal convincing? Why or whynot?

Chapter 2

1. John M. Hagedorn argues that rap music should be divid-edinto two categories. On the one hand, he describes how rap and hip hop music has been a way of expressing and developing identities of urban blacks; but on the other hand,he explains that rap music has also become an industry which glorifies thegangster lifestyle. He suggests that the first category has apositive influence on urban youth, while the second is negative and gives rapand hip hop a bad name. Do you think his categorization is accurate? Do you agree that there are different types of rap music with different socialvalues?

2. According to Terrance J. Taylor, more research is needed on therelationship between being a victim of a gang-related crime and joining agang. What obstacles do you see to this type of research?

3. After reading Michael Montgomery's and Ron Holvey's viewpoints about gangs and prisons, what do you think should be done to combat the problem ofgangs operating in prisons?

Chapter 3

1. Whose perspective do you think dominates Trymaine Lee's articleabout the police's reaction to Donnell McFarland's wake? Do youthink the accounts of the people he spoke to are accurate? In what ways maythese accounts be compromised?

2. After reading the viewpoints about gang prevention programs, what do youthink is the best way to evaluate the success of these programs? Howshould funders decide between supporting proven models for gang preventionprograms or backing innovative approaches?

3. Two different views on the potential of state lawmakers to prevent gangs are given in this chapter. Do you agree with Sarah Hammond'sarticle, which suggests that state lawmakers have an effective and multifacetedapproach to gang prevention, or do you agree with Judith Greene and Kevin Pranis that theactions of state lawmakers often actually exacerbate the gang problem?Why?

Chapter 4

1. The Fight Crime: Invest in Kids report identifies two ways in whichcitizens pay for gang crime: taxes that pay for the criminal justice system andprivate security costs. In what other ways might gang crime have a monetarycost to citizens?

2. After reading the articles on drugs and gangs, do you think if the UnitedStates was able to greatly reduce the number of people who use drugs thatwould also automatically improve the gang problem? Why or why not?

3. In Sarah Schmidt's viewpoint describing Catherine Bessette'sstudy on gang violence in Canadian high schools, how did Bessette gather herdata? What potential problems do you see with Bessette's data? Do you agree with her conclusions? Why or why not?

Organizations to Contact

The editors have compiled the following list of organizations concerned with the issues debated in this book. The descriptions are derived from materials provided by the organizations. All have publications or information available for interested readers. The list was compiled on the date of publication of the present volume; the information provided here may change. Be aware that many organizations take several weeks or longer to respond to inquiries, so allow as much time as possible.

American Civil Liberties Union (ACLU)
125 Broad St., 18th Floor, New York, NY   10004
(212) 549-2500 • fax: (212) 549-2646
e-mail: aclu@aclu.org
Web site: www.aclu.org

The ACLU is a national organization that works to defend Americans' civil rights as guaranteed by the U.S. Constitution. It opposes curfew laws for juveniles and others and seeks to protect the public-assembly rights of gang members or people associated with gangs. The ACLU publishes the biannual newsletter "Civil Liberties."

Boys & Girls Clubs of America
1275 W. Peachtree St. NE, Atlanta, GA   30309
(404) 487-5700
e-mail: info@bgca.org
Web site: www.bgca.org

Boys & Girls Clubs of America believes gangs form when boys and girls are left to find their own recreation and companionship in the streets. Its individual clubs throughout the United States "enhance the development of boys and girls by instilling a sense of competence, usefulness, belonging and influence." The organization's Targeted Outreach delinquency prevention program relies on referrals from schools, courts, law enforcement, and youth service agencies to recruit at-risk youths into ongoing club programs and activities.

Bridging Refugee Youth and Children's Services
3211 4th St. NE, Washington, DC   20017
(888) 572-6500
e-mail: info@brycs.org
Web site: www.brycs.org

Bridging Refugee Youth and Children's Services (BRYCS) is a an information-sharing network, administered by the U.S. Conference of Catholic Bishops/Migration and Refugee Services, to help refugee youth, children, and their families meet challenges of adjusting to life in the United States. Its Web site's publications clearinghouse offers many gang-prevention reports and articles, such as "Best Practices to Address Community Gang Problems."

Fight Crime: Invest in Kids
1212 New York Ave. NW, Suite 300, Washington, DC   20005
(202) 776-0027
e-mail: tturner@fightcrime.org
Web site: www.fightcrime.org

Fight Crime: Invest in Kids is a nonprofit anti-crime organization of more than 3,000 police chiefs, sheriffs, prosecutors, other law enforcement leaders, and violence survivors. The organization studies crime prevention strategies, informs the public and policy makers about those findings, and urges investment in programs proven to be effective. Programs supported include early education programs, prevention of child abuse and neglect, after-school programs for children and teens, and interventions to get troubled kids back on track.

Gang Alternatives Program
PO Box 408, San Pedro, CA   90733
(888) 293-9323 • fax: (310) 519-8730
e-mail: contact@gangfree.org

Web site: www.gangfree.org

The Gang Alternatives Program (GAP) was established to promote gang awareness in the Los Angeles area. Gangfree.org is its online national outreach program. GAP operates an outreach program for at-risk youth and referral and counseling services. It provides a school-based youth gang prevention curriculum for second, fourth, and sixth grades, a court-approved parent and teen education program, a graffiti prevention education program, and youth job training and development.

National Alliance of Gang Investigators' Associations

118 N. Lafayette, Brownsville, TN   38012
(731) 772-1395
Web site: www.nagia.org

The National Alliance of Gang Investigators Associations (NAGIA) is a network of criminal justice professionals, federal agencies, and other organizations dedicated to promoting anti-gang strategies. NAGIA advocates the standardization of anti-gang training, establishment of uniform gang definitions, assistance for communities with emerging gang problems, and input to policy makers. NAGIA also maintains an online library of articles on a variety of gang-related topics.

National Council on Crime and Delinquency (NCCD)

1970 Broadway, Suite 500, Oakland, CA   94612
(510) 208-0500 • fax: (510) 208-0511
www.nccd-crc.org

NCCD, founded in 1907, is a nonprofit organization that promotes effective, humane, fair, and economically sound solutions to family, community, and justice problems. The organization conducts research, promotes reform initiatives, and works with individuals, public and private organizations, and the media to prevent and reduce crime and delinquency. Two important areas of focus are youth violence and juvenile justice. NCCD's Web site offers many publications on these and other crime-related topics.

National Crime Prevention Council (NCPC)
2345 Crystal Dr., Suite 500, Arlington, VA   22202-4801
(202) 466-6272 • fax: (202) 296-1356
Web site: www.ncpc.org

NCPC provides training and other assistance to groups and individuals interested in crime prevention. It advocates job training and recreation programs as means to reduce youth crime and violence. The organization's Teens, Crime, and the Community (TCC) initiative has motivated more than one million young people to create safer schools and neighborhoods. TCC's Community Works program helps teens understand how crime affects them and their families, friends, and communities, and it involves them in crime prevention projects to help make their communities safer and more vital.

National Criminal Justice Reference Service
PO Box 6000, Rockville, MD   20849-6000
(800) 851-3420 • fax: (301) 519-5212
Web site: www.ncjrs.gov

The National Criminal Justice Reference Service is a federally funded resource offering justice and substance abuse information to support research, policy, and program development worldwide. The organization's Web site includes resources and statistics about gangs.

National School Safety Center
141 Duesenberg Dr., Suite 11, Westlake Village, CA   91362
(805) 373-9977 • fax: (805) 373-9277
Web site: www.schoolsafety.us

The National School Safety Center works to promote safety on college and university campuses. It develops training tools, strategies, and materials specific to the culture and safety needs of institutions of higher learning. It publishes the booklet *Gangs in Schools: Breaking Up Is Hard to Do*, the "School Safety Update" newsletter, and other books, videos, and papers on school safety topics.

National Youth Gang Center
PO Box 12729, Tallahassee, FL 32317-2729
(850) 385-0600 • fax: (850) 386-5356
e-mail: nygc@iir.com
Web site: www.iir.com/nygc/

The National Youth Gang Center (NYGC) is one of five major components of the Office of Juvenile Justice and Delinquency Prevention's (see below) response to the gang problem in the United States. The purpose of the NYGC is to help policy makers and practitioners reduce youth gang involvement and crime by providing information, resources, and practical tools to help develop and implement effective gang prevention, intervention, and suppression strategies.

National Youth Violence Prevention Resource Center
Sponsored by: Centers for Disease Control and Prevention
Atlanta, GA 30333
(800) 232-4636
Web site: www.safeyouth.org

The National Youth Violence Prevention Resource Center (NYVPRC) is a clearinghouse for communities working to prevent violence, including gang violence, committed by and against young people. The mission of NYVPRC is to provide local government leaders and community leaders with resources to help support their efforts to plan, develop, implement, and evaluate effective youth violence prevention efforts. NYVPRC is currently in the process of redirecting its mission to provide better online assistance and resources to help communities prevent gangs.

Office of Juvenile Justice and Delinquency Prevention (OJJDP)
810 Seventh St. NW, Washington, DC 20531
Web site: http://ojjdp.ncjrs.org

As the primary federal agency charged with monitoring and improving the juvenile justice system, the OJJDP develops and funds programs to prevent and control illegal drug use and serious crime by juveniles. Through its Juvenile Justice Clearinghouse, the OJJDP distributes the annual Youth Gang Survey and other fact sheets and reports. The office also sponsors the National Youth Gang Center (NYGC, see above) and several faith-based and community initiatives focused on at-risk youth and gang prevention.

Teens Against Gang Violence
2 Moody St., Dorchester, MA   02124
(617) 282-9659
e-mail: teensagv@aol.com
Web site: http://tagv.org

Teens Against Gang Violence (TAGV) is a volunteer, community-based, peer leadership program for teens. Its mission is to empower youth leaders by providing them with culturally appropriate knowledge, skills, tools, and relationships so they can educate others about nonviolence through peace and justice. TAGV distinguishes between gangs that are nonviolent and those that participate in violence. Through presentations and workshops, the TAGV educates teens, parents, schools, and community groups on violence, guns, and drug prevention.

Youth Crime Watch of America
9200 S. Dadeland Blvd., Suite 417, Miami, FL   33156
(305) 670-2409 • fax: (305) 670-3805
e-mail: ycwa@ycwa.org
Web site: www.ycwa.org

Youth Crime Watch of America (YCWA) is a nonprofit organization that assists students in developing youth-led programs, including crime and drug prevention programs, in communities and schools throughout the United States. Member-students at the elementary and secondary level help raise others' awareness of alcohol and drug abuse, crime, gangs, guns, and the importance of staying in school. Strategies include organizing student assemblies and patrols, conducting workshops, and challenging students to become personally involved in preventing crime and violence.

Bibliography of Books

Curt Bartol — *Juvenile Delinquency and Antisocial Behavior: A Developmental Perspective*. Upper Saddle River, NJ: Pearson Prentice Hall, 2009.

Ethan Brown — *Queens Reigns Supreme: Fat Cat, 50 Cent, and the Rise of the Hip Hop Hustler*. New York: Anchor, 2005.

Alex Caine — *Befriend and Betray: Infiltrating the Hells Angels, Bandidos and Other Criminal Brotherhoods*. New York: St. Martins Press, 2009.

Kyung-Seok Choo — *Gangs and Immigrant Youth*. New York: LFB Scholarly Pub. LLC, 2007.

Scott H. Decker — *European Street Gangs and Troublesome Youth Groups*. Lanham, MD: Alta Mira Press, 2005.

Rene Denfeld — *All God's Children: Inside the Dark and Violent World of Street Families*. Cambridge: PublicAffairs, 2007.

Tom Diaz — *No Boundaries: Transnational Latino Gangs and American Law Enforcement*. Ann Arbor, MI: University of Michigan Press, 2009.

Michel Dorais — *Gangs and Girls: Understanding Juvenile Prostitution*. Montreal: McGill-Queens University Press, 2009.

Michael Flynn   *Globalizing the Streets: Cross-Cultural Perspectives on Youth, Social Control, and Empowerment.* New York: Columbia University Press, 2008.

Robert J. Franzese   *Youth Gangs.* Springfield, IL: Charles C. Thomas, 2006.

Celeste Fremon   *G-Dog and the Homeboys: Father Greg Boyle and the Gangs of East Los Angeles.* Albuquerque: University of New Mexico Press, 2008.

Sarah Garland   *Gangs in Garden City: How Immigration, Segregation, and Youth Violence Are Changing America's Suburbs.* New York: Nation Books, 2009.

John M. Hagedorn   *Gangs in the Global City: Alternatives to Traditional Criminology.* Urbana: University of Illinois Press, 2007.

Tom Hayden   *Street Wars: Gangs and the Future of Violence.* New York: New Press, 2006.

Lorine A. Hughes   *Violent and Non-violent Disputes Involving Gang Youth.* New York: LFB Scholarly Pub. LLC, 2005.

————   *Studying Youth Gangs.* Lanham, MD: Alta Mira Press, 2006.

Bruce A. Jacobs   *Street Justice: Retaliation in the Criminal Underworld.* New York: Cambridge University Press, 2006.

Gareth Jones	*Youth Violence in Latin America: Gangs and Juvenile Justice in Perspective.* New York: Palgrave Macmillan, 2009.
Melvin Juette	*Wheelchair Warrior: Gangs, Disability, and Basketball.* Philadelphia: Temple University Press, 2009.
Charles M. Katz	*Policing Gangs in America.* New York: Cambridge University Press, 2006.
Malcolm Klein	*The Street Gangs of Euroburg: A Story of Research.* iUniverse Incorporated, 2009.
————	*Street Gang Patterns and Policies.* New York: Oxford University Press, 2006.
Samuel Logan	*This Is for the Mara Salvatrucha: Inside the MS-13, America's Most Violent Gang.* New York: Hyperion, 2009.
Spring Miller	*No Place to Hide: Gang, State, and Clandestine Violence in El Salvador.* Cambridge, MA: Human Rights Program at Harvard Law School, 2009.
William Queen	*Under and Alone: The True Story of the Undercover Agent Who Infiltrated America's Most Violent Outlaw Motorcycle Gang.* New York: Ballantine Books, 2007.
Tony Rafael	*The Mexican Mafia.* New York: Encounter Books, 2007.

Luis J. Rodriguez   *Always Running: La Vida Loca.* New York: Touchstone, 2005.

James F. Short, Jr.   *Studying Youth Gangs.* Lanham, MD: Alta Mira Press, 2006.

Debra Smith   *Literacy and Advocacy in Adolescent Family, Gang, School, and Juvenile Court Communities.* Mahwah, NJ: Lawrence Erlbaum Associates, 2006.

Karen Umemoto   *The Truce: Lessons from an L.A. Gang War.* Ithaca: Cornell University Press, 2006.

Avelardo Valdez   *Mexican American Girls and Gang Violence: Beyond Risk.* New York: Palgrave Macmillan, 2009.

Frank van Gemert   *Street Gangs, Migration and Ethnicity.* Portland, OR: Willan, 2008.

Sudhir Venkatesh   *Gang Leader for a Day: A Rogue Sociologist Takes to the Streets.* New York: Penguin, 2008.

James Diego Vigil   *The Projects: Gang and Non-gang Families in East Los Angeles.* Austin: University of Texas Press, 2007.

Index

A

Adolescent development, 62–64
Afrika Bambaataa, 81–83
Agley, Arlene, 64
Aguilar, Alfonso, 47
Al-Qaeda, 48
Anti-Gang Act, 114
Aragon Elementary School, 184, 186–187
Aryan Brotherhood, 42
Associated Press, 57

B

Ballou, Brian, 45–50
BBC (British Broadcasting Corporation), 31
Bennett, Trevor, 173–182
Bessette, Catherine, 189–191
Black Gangster Disciples, 164
Bloods, 164–165
Booth, Nate, 42, 44
British Broadcasting Corporation (BBC), 31
Brown, Devon, 106
Browne, Paul, 130
Bureau of Alcohol, Tobacco, Firearms and Explosives, 46
Bureau of International Law Enforcement Affairs, 161
Bushwick Community High School, 132

C

Calderón, Felipe, 14
California Department of Corrections, 42
California legislation, 114–115
California Mexican Mafia, 77, 91
Cameron, David, 58
CAPS (Chicago Alternative Policing System), 139
Carillio, Louis, 186–187
CCDAP (Cook County Department of Adult Probation), 138–139
Center for the Study and Prevention of Violence, 151
Centre for Urban Schooling, 191
Chelsea Collaborative, 49
Chicago Alternative Policing System (CAPS), 139
Chicago Department of Human Services, 139
Chicago gangs, 164–165
Chicago Police Department (CPD), 138–139
Chicanos Por Vida (CPV), 22
Claiming My City (music CD), 47
Clark, Frank, 109
Cleaver, Eldridge, 86
Clinkscales, Keith, 88
Clinton, Bill, 87
Coalition for Evidence-Based Policy, 157
Collord, George, 96–98
Community mobilization, 144–145

resources, 37–38, 102–104, 144–145

risk factors, 64

Community Oriented Policing Service (COPS), 185

Comprehensive Gang Program Model, Office of Juvenile Justice and Delinquency Prevention, 123–124

Congressional Black Caucus, 40

Congressional Missing and Exploited Children Caucus, 173

Cook County Department of Adult Probation (CCDAP), 138

COPS (Community Oriented Policing Service), 185

Cortina, Epitacio, 91–92

CPD (Chicago Police Department), 138–139

Crazy Girl Nortenas, 26

Crews, cliques, posses, 167

Crime statistics, United Kingdom, 52–53, 179

Crime trends, costs, 168

Crips, 164–165

Cummings, Elijah, 109

CVP (Chicanos Por Vida), 22

D

Daily News (newspaper), 161

Daley, Richard J., 82

DARE (Drug Abuse Resistance Education), 155–157

Decker, Scott, 62

Dole, Bob, 87

The Dominion Post (newspaper), 162

Donovan, Kevin, 83–84

Drug abuse, 35, 178, 180–182

Drug Abuse Resistance Education (DARE), 155–157

Drug trafficking, 170–174

DuBois, W. E. B., 86

E

East Coast Gang Investigators Association (ECGIA), 110

East Europeans, 52–53

The Economist (magazine), 16, 51–54

Education, 109–110, 115

Elizabeth Fry Society, 31

Elliot, Delbert, 150–158

Entertainment, media, 58, 78–79

Erickson, Erik, 62

Evening Standard (newspaper), 58

Ex-gang members, 38–39

F

Fairbanks, Mike, 22–24, 26

Family risk factors, 64

Farrakahn, Louis, 87

Federal Bureau of Investigation (FBI), statistics, 112

Federal Collaboration on What Works, 157

Federal prosecutors, 60

Female gangs, 22–27
    changes, 22–23
    evidence, 30–32
    membership, community types, 24
    violence statistics, 31

Fight Crime: Invest in Kids, 163–169

Flaccus, Gillian, 41–44

Flores, Ely, 34–40

Foreign prison inmates, 53

Fox, James, 164
Frias, Aramando, Jr., 90, 97

G

Gallagher, Kathleen, 191
Gang Awareness and Prevention
  Program (GAPP), 104–105
Gang Awareness Suppression and
  Prevention Program (GASPP),
  109
Gang prevention, control
    effectiveness, 150–158
    evaluated programs outcomes,
      154–155
    evidence-based programs,
      151–152, 156–158
    funding, 152–153, 155–156
    objectives, 119
    Operation Ceasefire, 120–121
    police gang units, 124–127
    problems, 121–124
    program evaluation, 152–154
    program promotion, 157–158
    program selection, 151
    research, 123
    school-based programs, 152
    targets, 119–120
    unproven programs funding,
      155–156
    untested programs, 152
Gang Reduction & Aggressive Su-
  pervised Parole (GRASP), 104
Gang(s)
    attraction, 61–63, 112–113
    cities, 167
    crews, cliques, posses, 167
    crime trends, costs, 168–169
    culture, 75–77
    family support, 57–58
    FBI statistics, 112
    growth, 164–165

    history, 61, 165
    international, 14
    local, 77, 82–83
    mentality, 74–75
    middle class, 42–43
    national, 77
    prevention, 60–62, 104–105
    risk factors, 63–64
    rural areas, 167
    stereotypes, 176
    suburbs, 19–20, 167
    traditional, 165, 167
    types, 165, 176
    U.S. *vs.* UK, 176, 179–180
Gansta rap, 86–88
GAPP (Gang Awareness and Pre-
  vention Program), 104–105
GASPP (Gang Awareness Suppres-
  sion and Prevention Program),
  109
Gilhooly, Michael, 46
Gilroy, Paul, 86
Gohmert, Louie, 16
Gonzalez, Eloisa, 22–27
Gore, Bobby, 83
Graffiti, 115–116
GRASP (Gang Reduction & Ag-
  gressive Supervised Parole), 104
Greene, Judith, 117–127
GVRP (Little Village Gang Vio-
  lence Reduction Project)
    author role, 139
    community mobilization,
      144–145
    contact between groups, 140–
      142
    data interpretation, 148–149
    entering the field, 139–140
    evaluation-research, 141
    local residents, 143
    NAGV, 145–146

project formation, 138–139
self-reported offense changes,
148
social context changes, 146–
147
youth-worker outreach, 142–
143

H

Hagedorn, John, 80–88
Hammond, Sarah, 111–116
Hancock, Susannah, 32
Hip Hop Matters (Watkins), 83
Hip-hop
Afrika Bambaataa, 81–84
cultural influences, 85–86
culture, 81, 85
elements, 81
gangs, history, 81–83
identity, self recognition, 85
lyrics, 77–78
types, 81
Holloway, Katy, 173–182
Holvey, Ron, 99–106
Home videos, 78
Homicide, type by age, 166
Hope Gardens housing project,
131
House Subcommittee on Healthy
Families and Communities, 109
Houston, 171–173
Howell, James "Buddy," 64
Hurst, Christopher, 114

I

Identity theft, 43–44
Illinois Criminal Justice Information Authority (ICJIA), 138

Immigrants, immigration, 16, 47
crime, 51–54
Great Britain, 51–54
illegal, 46–49
Immigration and Customs Enforcement agency, 46
Individual risk factors, 64

J

Jones, Jerrauld, 57
Juvenile delinquency, 164
Juvenile poverty, crime, 37

K

Katz, Charles, 124–127
Korem, Dan, 19
Kyes, Brian, 46

L

LA CAUSA (Los Angeles Commu-
nities Advocating for Unity, So-
cial Justice, and Action), 38–40
La Krazy Criminals, 26
Lampson, Nicholas, 170–174
Latin Kings, 13, 146–147, 164
Latino Caucus, 40
Law enforcement, 137
community education, 109
corruption, 161–162
gang units, 124–126
UK, 53–54
Lee, Trymaine, 128–133
Legislation, 173–174
Leventhal, Robert, 161
Life Skills Training, 157
Linden Street Bloods, 131–132
Lindsay, John, 82

Little Village Gang Violence Reduction Project (GVRP)
  author role, 139
  community mobilization, 144–145
  contact between groups, 140–142
  data interpretation, 148–149
  entering the field, 139–140
  evaluation-research, 141
  local residents, 143
  NAGV, 145–146
  project formation, 138–139
  self-reported offense changes, 148
  social context changes, 146–147
  youth-worker outreach, 142–143
LL Cool J., 84
Los Angeles Communities Advocating for Unity, Social Justice, and Action (LA CAUSA), 38–40
Los Angeles gangs, 164
Los Angeles Sentinel (newspaper), 19–20
Los Angeles Unified School District, 186
Los Zetas, 16
Lovebug Starski, 82
Lyddanne, Donald, 73–79

M

MacMillan, Paul, 47
Make the Road by Walking, 135
Mara Salvatrucha (MS-13), 46–50, 167
Marquez, Robert, 93
Maryland Department of Juvenile Services, 109

Mazza, Donald "Popeye," 42
MBTA (Massachusetts Bay Transportation Authority), 46
McBride, Wes, 76–77
McFarland, Donnell, 130–135
McGrath, Joseph, 91
Mean Girls (radio), 31
Media, entertainment, 58, 78–79, 82
Mendoza, Tony, 115
Mexico
  drug gangs, 14–17
  Los Zetas, 16
  U.S. aid, 15–16
Middle class, 42–43
Middlesex Sheriff's Department, 46
Miller, Jody, 23, 25–27
Montgomery, Michael, 89–98
Moore, Wayne, 186
MS-13 (Mara Salvatrucha), 46–50, 167
Mulitalo, Chris, 57

N

NAGV (Neighbors Against Gang Violence), 145–146
National Center for Missing and Exploited Children (NCMEC), 173
National Drug Intelligence Center (NDIC), 171–173
National Post (newspaper), 15
National Youth Gang Center (NYGC), 64
National Youth Gang Survey, 164–165
Nazi Low Riders, 42

NCMEC (National Center for Missing and Exploited Children), 173

NDIC (National Drug Intelligence Center), 171–173

Neighborhood risk factors, 64

Neighbors Against Gang Violence (NAGV), 145–146

New English and Welsh Arrestee Drug Abuse Monitoring (NEW-DAM), 177

New Jersey Department of Corrections (NJDOC), 99–106

New Orleans, 171

New York Times (newspaper), 19

NEW-ADAM (New English and Welsh Arrestee Drug Abuse Monitoring), 177

North Side Villains, 26

Nuestro Familia (NF), 89–92, 95–98

NYGC (National Youth Gang Center), 64

O

Office of Gang and Youth Violence Policy, 115

Office of Juvenile Justice and Delinquency Prevention, 123

Operation 13 (Thirteen), 46

Operation Ceasefire, 120–121

Operation Community Shield, 47

Orange County Probation Department, 43

Organized Crime Digest, 19

Ortiz, Jim, 25–26

P

Parents, parental responsibility, 57–58, 105, 115

Peavy, Ray, 119

Peer groups, 62, 64

Pelican Bay State Prison, 90–93

Play Gift Surenas, 26

Police gang control units, 124–127

Policing Gangs in America (Katz, Webb), 124

Pranis, Kevin, 117–127

Pretty Boy Family, 131–132, 135

Prisons, prison gangs, 77
  controlling, 100–106
  corruption, 161–162
  foreign inmates, 53
  NF, 89–92, 95–98
  proliferation, 89–98
  solitary confinement, 103
  three-part management program, 101–102

Prosecutorial Tools Improvement Act, 173–174

Public Enemy No. 1, 41
  Aryan Brotherhood, 42–43
  identity theft, 43–44
  origins, activities, 43–44

Q

Quebec Department of Education, 190

Queen Latifah, 84

R

Rap industry, 73–88

Rappers Delight (song), 82

Risk factors, 63–64

Ritter, Susan, 50

Rochester Youth Development Study, 179

Rose, Tricia, 85

Rosenblatt, Susannah, 183–187

S

Sacchett, Maria, 45–50

Salas, Marcos, 184–185

Salinas, 85, 93

Santana, Arturo, 24

Schmidt, Sarah, 188–191

Schools, school violence, 184–187, 189–191

Schumer, Charles, 185

Schwarzenegger, Arnold, 94

Security Threat Group Management Unit (STGMU), 102, 105–106

Self-worth, 61

Shaw, Jamiel, 112

Slaten, Steve, 42

Smith, Joan, 28–33

Smith, Lowell, 43

Social belonging, 59–65

Social issues, 29–30, 36–38

Solis, Hilda, 39

Soul on Ice (Cleaver), 86

South Central L.A., 36

Spergel, Irving, 136–149

St. Louis Anti-Gang Initiative, 122

Start Taking Alcohol Risks Seriously (STARS), 156

State legislation, 113–116

STGMU (Security Threat Group Management Unit), 102, 105–106

Street gangs, defined, 176

Suburban Gangs (Korem), 19

Suburbs, gang presence, 19–20

Sugar Hill Gang, 82

T

Target Practice (music CD), 96

Taylor, Terrance, 66–72

Terrorism, 174

The Theatre of Urban: Youth and Schooling in Dangerous Times (Gallagher), 191

Time Warner, 82

Two Six, 139, 146–147

U

United Kingdom (UK), 51–54, 176, 179–180

The United Press International, 161

United States (U.S.)
 aid to Mexico, 15–16
 crime statistics, 179–180
 illegal drug market, 14
 U.K. *vs.*, 179–180

US Conference of Mayors, 40

US Department of Labor Youth-Build program, 38, 40

US Office of Citizenship, 47

V

Van Winkle, Barrik, 62

Vibe (magazine), 88

Vice Lords, 164

Victims, victimization, 67–69
 boys, 71–72
 girls, 70–71
 prior to gang membership, 70–71
 protection, 70–71
 research, 67–71
 stages, 67–68
 students, 190
 violence, 68–69

Violence, 44, 95, 169
    culture, life, 35–36
    girl gangs, 31
    men *vs.* women, 30
    Mexican drug gangs, 14–15
    victims, victimization, 68–69

W

Washington Irving Middle School, 185–186
Washington State Institute for Public Policy, 158
Washington state legislation, 113–114
Washington Times (newspaper), 15
Watkins, S. Craig, 83
Weapons, 36
Webb, Vincent, 124–127
West, Cornel, 85
West Side Story (musical), 176

Wilberg, Wayne, 165
Woman's Hour (radio), 31–32
Working Groups on Girls (WGGs), 31
WUNR 1600 AM (radio), 49
Wyrick, Phelan, 59–63

Y

Yakima County gangs, 22–27
Yorty, Samuel, 82
Youth Impact, 57
Youth Justice Board, 32–33
Youth Justice Coalition, 38
Youth workers, 142–143
YouthBuild USA, 38
Youth-gang related homicides, 164, 166

Z

Zulu Nation, 84